Deleted

The Book of Maidstone 1981
has been published as a Limited
Edition of which
this is

Number

A complete list of the
original subscribers is
printed at the back of the book

THE BOOK OF
MAIDSTONE

FRONT COVER: The Palace at Maidstone, c1740.

The Old Palace and All Saints Church, c1910.

THE BOOK OF MAIDSTONE

Kent's County Town

BY

HILARY C. WATSON MA

BARRACUDA BOOKS LIMITED
BUCKINGHAM, ENGLAND
MCMLXXXI

PUBLISHED BY BARRACUDA BOOKS
LIMITED
BUCKINGHAM, ENGLAND
AND PRINTED BY
AYLESBURY LITHOPRINT LIMITED
AYLESBURY, ENGLAND

BOUND BY
WEATHERBY WOOLNOUGH
WELLINGBOROUGH, ENGLAND

JACKET PRINTED BY
CHENEY & SONS LIMITED
BANBURY, OXON

LITHOGRAPHY BY
D. C. LITHO LIMITED
BANBURY, OXON

DISPLAY SET IN BASKERVILLE
& TEXT SET IN 10/11PT BASKERVILLE BY
PERFORMANCE TYPESETTING LIMITED
MILTON KEYNES, ENGLAND

© Hilary C. Watson 1981

ISBN 0 86023 121 6

Contents

Bibliography

Abell, H.F. 'Kent and the Great Civil War', *The Kentish Express 1901*
Austen, B. *English Provincial Posts* Phillimore 1978
Bushell, T.A. Barracuda Guide to County History Vol I: *Kent* 1976
Cave-Brown, J. *History of the Parish Church of All Saints Maidstone* Bunyard/Burgiss Brown
Copley, G.J. *An Archaeology of South East England* Phoenix 1958
Crouch, M. *Kent* Batsford 1966
Everitt, A.M. *The Community of Kent and the Great Rebellion 1640-60* Leicester University Press 1966
Holloway, R. *The Queen's Own Royal West Kent Regiment* Leo Cooper 1973
Goodsall, R.H. *A Kentish Patchwork* Constable 1966
Jerrold, W *Highways and Byways in Kent* Macmillan 1924
Jessup, F.W. *A History of Kent* Darwin Finlayson 1959
Jessup, F.W. *Kent History Illustrated* Kent County Council 1966
Lamb, J.W. *The Archbishopric of Canterbury* The Faith Press 1971
Mee, A. *Kent* 10th ed, Hodder and Stoughton 1961 (1st published 1936)
Muggeridge, S.J. *The Postal History of Maidstone* Postal History Society 1972
Newman, J. *West Kent and The Weald* Penguin 1969
Russell, J.M. *The History of Maidstone* William Vivish 1881
Thomas, G.T. *Fire Fighting in Maidstone* Phillimore 1976
Wright, C. *Kent Through the Years* Batesford 1975
Worssam, B.C. *Geology of the country around Maidstone* HMSO 1963
Archaeologia Cantiana 1858. . .
Guide to the Kent County Archives Office 1st Supplement 1957-1968 Kent County Council.
Kent Police 1857-1957 Published J.A. Jennings Ltd Canterbury 1957
Maidstone Grammar School 1549-1949 Alabaster Passmore and Sons Ltd.
Records of Maidstone William Hobbs and Sons Ltd Maidstone 1926
The Southern Way with Water Southern Water Authority 1976
Victoria County History Vols I   II   III Archibald Constable and Co 1908

Key to Caption Credits

KCA	Kent County Archives
KCL	Kent County Library
MBC	Maidstone Borough Council
MC	Mansell Collection
MM	Maidstone Museums and Art Gallery
R	Russell's *History of Maidstone* 1881

Foreword

by Gordon Bonner F.R.I.B.A.
Leader – Maidstone Borough Council

It is a privilege to be invited to contribute a foreword to this book, particularly as the subject is one which is very dear to my own heart.

Maidstone is a fascinating town with a long and varied history, and all those who live and work in the Borough have every reason to be proud of its rich heritage. This new, informative book is very welcome and will be keenly demanded.

Although Hilary Watson has a uniquely wide knowledge of her subject, the compilation of this book must have required wide and intensive research. It is, therefore, a work of true scholarship but, at the same time, is presented in a concise and sufficiently comprehensive manner for the purposes of the general reader.

I cannot suppose that such an interesting and authentic account of Maidstone, the centre of a County famous in history requires any recommendation to you, but I am confident that the contents of this book will not only excite the curiosity but create a deeper understanding of the history of our town. I hope that all who read it, visitors and Maidstonians alike, will enjoy and profit from it.

Introduction

I have written this book for enjoyment as well as for information. Maidstone has been associated with many significant events, and a County Town with such a heritage will surely maintain its importance. It is 100 years since the last full length history of Maidstone was published. I have attempted to extend the information already researched, and to correct many of the false notions of earlier authors. New information is constantly emerging so I cannot guarantee to be infallible. However, I hope that in this year of the 600th anniversary of the Peasants Revolt—the events of which so involved the Town—the people of Maidstone will feel they have *their* history of *their* town.

Acknowledgements

I wish to thank the numerous people who gave me information and advice. Please forgive me if your name is unwittingly omitted. In particular, grateful thanks are due to the instigators of European Heritage Year, who sparked off the idea for this book; the Members of the Maidstone Society for unerring encouragment, and Kent Archaeological Society whose journal is so valuable. I am deeply indebted to L.R.A. Grove and all the staff of Maidstone Museums and Art Gallery, especially G. Hunter, D. Kelly and Ms V. Tonge. Thanks go also to the management and staff of Maidstone Town Library and Kent County Library, Springfield. I could not have managed without Kent County Archives or many of the staff of Maidstone Borough Council. I am also indebted to Mrs V. Conway, S. Green, G. Horrocks and P. Oldham.

Dedication

for my parents

In Madum's Vale

This maketh me at home to hunt and hawk
And in foul weather at my book to sit . . .
But here I am in Kent and Christendom
Among the muses where I read and rhyme

> Sir Thomas Wyatt   (from *Satires*)

Yeomen and countrymen, attend my song:
Whether you shiver in the marshy Weald,
Egregious shepherds of unnumber'd flocks,
Whose fleeces, poison'd into purple, deck
All Europe's kings: or in fair Madum's vale
Imparadis'd, blest denizons, ye dwell;

> Christopher Smart (from *The Hop Garden*)

ABOVE: Kits Coty as depicted in 1828. BELOW: Lower
Kits Coty, also known as the Countless Stones because of
their jumbled formation.

Of Stones and Men

The town of Maidstone is a late development when compared with the age of the Wealden rocks in the area. The hundred million years old upper strata of south east England and northern France were covered by a large lake. Layers of sand and clay were laid down, and later over a long period the shells of minute sea creatures formed the chalk of the North Downs over the Wealden deposit.

It was during this period (one hundred million years ago) that dinosaurs roamed the area, leaving footprints in the soft mud. In 1834 the fossil remains of an iguanadon were discovered in a quarry off Queens Road, Maidstone, by W.H. Benstead. This discovery caused much interest at the time and as a consequence an iguanadon was added as a supporter to the Borough of Maidstone coat of arms in 1949.

The first human inhabitants of the Maidstone area were of the Palaeolithic Age. They had come west across the land that then linked Britain to Europe. Their simple stone tools have survived on the North Downs and in the river gravels at nearby Aylesford. The only animal remains from this age belonged to wild creatures such as the mammoth, a tooth of which was found on the site of Barclay's Bank in Maidstone High Street in 1959.

Mesolithic man improved his tools, making full use of the flints readily available in the local chalk, to produce implements and axes which have retained their sharpness into modern times.

Neolithic man left more obvious evidence of his habitation by building large burial chambers between 35,000 BC and 25,000 BC long before the erection of Stonehenge in about 1900 BC to 1700 BC. These large earth mounds usually measured 200 to 300 feet in length, 30 to 40 feet in width and between 15 and 20 feet in height. In shape they were either a long oval or of a shorter squarish form.

Normally, in the east end of these mounds were burial chambers, the earth being retained by large boulders. In this space human remains were placed, perhaps from a community or just a single family. When the Chestnuts chamber at Addington, (seven miles from Maidstone) was recently excavated, the cremated remains of ten Neolithic people were found. Around each mound was a peristalith, (circle of stones), which has often collapsed or been removed.

In the Maidstone area these megaliths were sited on the south side of the North Downs. The best preserved example may be seen on the west side of the Medway valley near Trottiscliffe, where the Coldrum barrow and peristalith stand. A mile south of this site at Addington are the remains of two barrows. The first was some 200 feet long with some surrounding stones, (the Addington to Wrotham Heath Road cutting through the whole barrow,) the second shorter barrow called Chestnuts.

On the east side of the Medway valley, only the stones used in earthworks remain. The most famous is Kits Coty House, a group of four stones which is either the remains of a burial chamber or a false entrance to the long barrow.

Five hundred yards to the south is Lower Kits Coty House which is also aptly known as the Countless Stones. The twenty or so stones collapsed into their present state during the early part of the eighteenth century. They narrowly missed complete destruction in 1836 when it was proposed that they be used to pave the barracks at Sheerness.

There is evidence of other earthworks. Just to the east of Lower Kits Coty stood Smythe's megalith, named after the Town Clerk of Maidstone, Clement Taylor Smythe, who studied its form when it was discovered in 1836. This feature has since merged once more into the landscape. In 1844 several stones, each having a peristalith, were studied in the area above Kits Coty House. Half a mile to the west of Lower Kits Coty House the possible remains of two stone circles have been noted, though whether they date from the Stone Age or were gathered together to make field ploughing easier in a more recent age is uncertain.

Single stones like the 17th century Jostling stone, which was situated above Boxley, and the White Horse Stone near Lower Kits Coty) may sometimes have been connected with Neolithic culture although their close proximity to the Pilgrim's Way suggests some may be markers for this prehistoric trackway.

The rock used for all these stones is known as sarsen. This hard silicified sandstone came from strata known as the Reading Beds, which lay above the chalk layers. This rock was eroded away, only small areas remaining, from which the stones used in the construction of burial chambers and monuments were taken.

Neolithic man used small flint stones to produce more complex tools than his predecessors. Examples of flint arrowheads and axeheads have been found over a wide area, but more especially on the higher ground of Barming, Bearsted and Boxley.

About 1800 BC, people from the areas of the Netherlands and Germany came into Kent across the now water-submerged land bridge. They have been given the name of Beaker People from the distinctive type of drinking cup they placed beside their dead. Such pottery has been found near the Cherry Tree and Upper Fant Road Barming, near Kits Coty House, and along the Ashford Road.

The most important innovation the Beaker people brought was

bronze, a combination of (soft) tin and (brittle) copper which produced the first metal which could easily be formed into strong implements. Bronze axe heads have been found on Blue Bell Hill, and beside the Sutton Road to the south of Maidstone. A more spectacular find of four

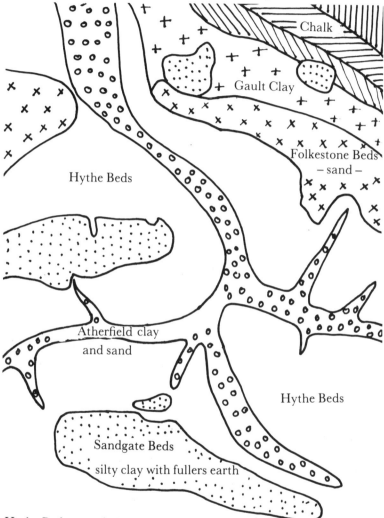

Chalk

Gault Clay

Folkestone Beds
– sand –

Hythe Beds

Atherfield clay
and sand

Hythe Beds

Sandgate Beds

silty clay with fullers earth

Hythe Beds – sandy limestone and calcareaus sand

A geological sketch map of the Maidstone area.

gold armlets, (one of which was incomplete), was made in the Medway below Aylesford in 1861.

The knowledge of how to work the hard metal iron was brought across the Channel circa 500-450 BC. Small deposits of ironstone in the

Lenham Beds to the north east of Maidstone and on top of the North Downs above Harrietsham and Hollingbourne may have provided the raw material for iron tools and weapons found locally.

The majority of Iron Age remains are pottery fragments, such as those found in the cemetery of this period at Aylesford, which also produced a wooden bucket with bronze banding and decoration – now in the British Museum, London. A stone quern found beside Scrubbs Lane, Maidstone, illustrates the agricultural improvements made during the Iron Age.

In 55BC Julius Caesar began the Roman invasions but real colonisation did not commence until AD 43 when Aulus Plautus landed on the east coast of Kent.

The nearest Roman town to Maidstone was at Rochester, the road from which ran to the port of Lympne, via Maidstone's Stone Street. The area around Maidstone supported a moderately sized farming community with several villas. An earthwork which stood by the Sutton Road at Mangravet is thought to have been a cattle compound of this period.

Villas, normally farming complexes, were built just above the Medway near the present sites of Barming Church, Maidstone East Station, Allington Castle, and along the Roman Stone Street such as that near the site of the present Boys' Grammar School.

A Romano-British refuse tip in Buckland Hill has produced pottery fragments, and artifacts such as a glass flask, part of a pair of dividers, a bronze brooch and statuettes of Roman gods have been found over a wide area. The largest hoard of coins in the town (57 in number) was found in Wyke Manor Road.

In 407 AD the last of the Roman Legions left Britain to protect their homeland from attack by the Goths but there is evidence that some remnants of Roman civilization remained until at least the middle of the 5th century.

However, the government of Britain gradually disintegrated into warring factions. Tradition says that eventually a leader, Vortigern, was chosen but even he seemed powerless. In 449 he invited two federate Jutish leaders Hengist and Horsa, to fight for him in return for land, possibly the Isle of Thanet. They accepted and all was successful with Vortigern marrying Hengist's daughter in 450. Hengist then proclaimed himself king and encouraged his compatriots from Jutland to settle in his British kingdom. This angered the indigenous people and war broke out. One of the fiercest battles took place in 455 at Aylesford where Catigern, one of Vortigern's sons, and Horsa killed each other. Eventually the Britons were driven from Kent, just as the Angles and Saxons were taking over adjoining counties.

Gradually the county of Kent evolved, and when in 560 Ethelbert became the Bretwalda of Kent, his kingdom extended north to the Humber. He was married to a Frankish princess, whose Christian religion encouraged Ethelbert to give hospitality to St Augustine in 597. The area was not immediately converted to Christianity.

In 841 the heathen Norse invaders raided Rochester, and are said to have ventured inland to the comparatively unprosperous Allington.

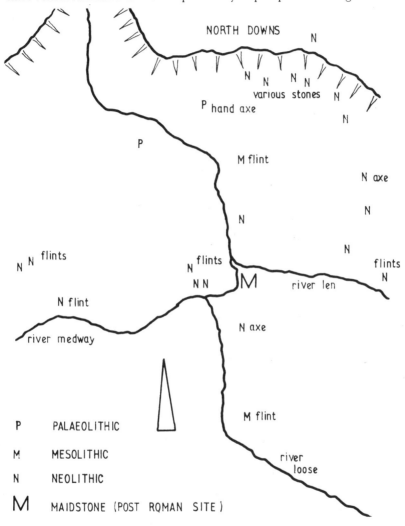

NORTH DOWNS

N

N N   N N
various stones N

P hand axe

N

P

M flint

N axe

N

N

N

N N flints   flints   flints
N   N
N N   M river len

N flint

N axe

river medway

M flint

P   PALAEOLITHIC

M   MESOLITHIC   river
                          loose
N   NEOLITHIC

M   MAIDSTONE (POST ROMAN SITE)

A sketch map showing the distribution of pre-historic remains in the Maidstone area.

Archaeological finds from this time are mostly burial remains. Glass beads and weapons were found with skeletons at Hollingbourne in 1847, and a similar discovery on the east side of Wheeler Street, Maidstone in 1836 revealed a sixth century silver gilt brooch with garnets and blue stones. More recently, in 1946 a sixth century burial site containing the remains of two men and a woman were found at Lenham.

A change to Christian practices took place during the seventh century. This is demonstrated locally by an eighth century gold cross found at Thurnham.

In 973 Edgar, the first King of all England ascended to the throne bringing the House of Wessex to power. At last England was unified as a powerful Christian nation. In January of 1066 Edgar's grandson, King Edward the Confessor, died. Edward's nephew Harold Godwinson, the Earl of Kent, was elected King of England. The following October William, Duke of Normandy, greedy for power, and related to Edward through the female line, contested the decision to make Harold king, claiming that Edward wanted him to have the Crown. With his army and his half brother, whom he had made Bishop of Bayeux, he invaded England. At the Battle of Hastings a tired English army – just returned from defeating a northern threat – were soundly beaten by the Norman force. William rewarded Odo, (who had wielded his bishop's mace instead of a sword at the battle), with the Earldom of Kent, and some 200 Kentish manors scattered throughout the county. Odo was not satisfied, and by 1076 had seized land belonging to the Sees of Rochester and Canterbury, including the manor of Maidstone. Lanfranc, Archbishop of Canterbury appealed to the self-crowned William, who appointed the aged Bishop Aegelric of Selsey, who understood Anglo-Saxon law, and the Norman Bishop of Coutances, to preside over a court. The trial was held on Penenden Heath, which has the tradition of being a meeting place since earliest times, and was also a central point for the county. After three days the decision was made in favour of Lanfranc. Odo turned his attentions elsewhere; in 1082 he tried to seek the Papacy. He returned to reclaim his lands after William's death, but was finally banished for raising a rebellion against King William Rufus.

In 1086 the land owners of Kent were called to attend a shiremote held on Penenden Heath, where they had to give information concerning their lands, which was to form part of the Domesday Book. This survey enabled William I to discover the extent of his kingdom, and was to make administrative duties, such as tax gathering, more simple. The Domesday Book provides the historian with a picture of early Maidstone. The settlement was a manor which belonged to the Archbishop of Canterbury, it was moderately sized and a little larger than the nearby settlements of Hollingbourne and East Farleigh.

Maidstone was listed as having had a church, six mills and an agricultural community of 57 villeins (tenants who worked their rented area of land), 31 bordars (tenants with a small amount of land), and 20 serfs who were little better than slaves. The cultivated land measured ten sulungs, a sulung being the area that an eight ox plough team could work over a year, the exact area varying according to the quality of the soil. For Maidstone it has been estimated that one sulung was about 160 acres, giving a total of 1,600 acres. By comparison, Dartford comprised 4,234 acres, worked by 55 ox teams. The recorded

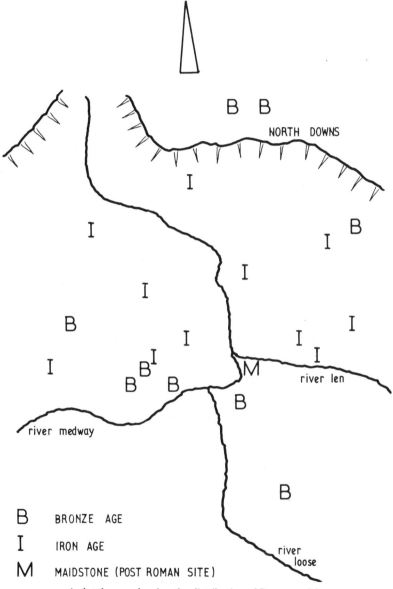

A sketch map showing the distribution of Bronze and Iron Age remains in the area around Maidstone.

population numbered 155, (excluding women, children, and the priest).

Three knights leased four sulungs of land from the Archbishop, and also took two thirds of the eels caught at the two fisheries, and had use of two salt pans.

The name given to this community living off the land was spelt Medestan or Meddestane in the Domesday Book. A later document noting the villages which gave payment to maintain Rochester bridge, (Textus Roffensis c1115) gave the name as Maegthanstane. This variety of spellings reflects the lack of uniform spelling at the time, which often relied on pronunciation.

The meaning of the town's name is now generally agreed not to mean the town on or by the Medway. It could perhaps mean maiden's stone, a standing stone of the neolithic period, but the town is rather far from the North Downs where such a stone would have been procured. The explanation that it means a meeting place of the Maegdan tribe is tenuous. A possibility is that the 'Maid . . . ' and its earlier forms are a corruption of 'mere' which was the term for an unploughed strip between each man's area of land, and came to describe a boundary. This fits in with the period of the first settlement on the site; earlier pre-Romano-)British remains are concentrated on the surrounding high ground and not in the marshy river valley. The 'stone' part of the name may well refer to the relatively high firm ground above the Medway on which the Archbishops built their church and manor house. Or it could refer to a stone used as a boundary marker, though a boundary of what or where is not clear.

At first the meeting place of Penenden Heath, below the North Downs, appears to have been the more obvious place for a successful settlement. It was above soft ground, considered to be the centre of the county, and was regularly visited by the judicial courts.

Maidstone, being a manor of the Archbishop of Canterbury, automatically attained a certain degree of importance. It was in a sheltered position, and the soil was suitable for cultivation. The rivers of Medway, Len and Loose had shaped the land into a defensible stronghold and also provided power to drive water mills. Maidstone was at the crossroads of a Roman road, and a trackway which ran east-west, (Bearsted to Barming) and crossed the Medway at Maidstone where the river was not as marshy as at Aylesford.

Gradually the importance of Maidstone was to increase, with the transference of the county administration into the town centre from Penenden Heath, and the building of a grand ecclesiastical Manor House, College and Church, to form a powerful combination of Crown and Church influence.

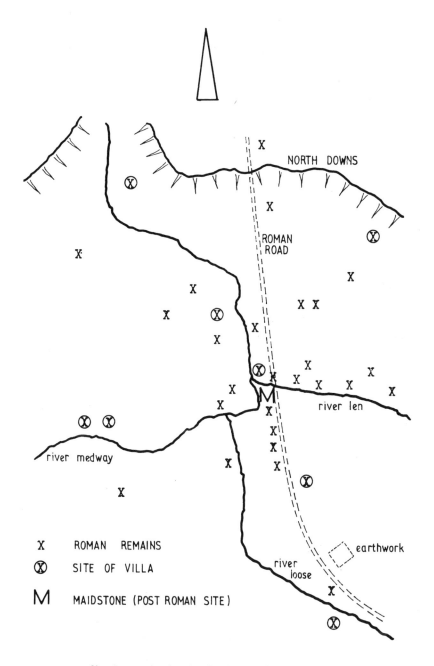

NORTH DOWNS

ROMAN
ROAD

river len

river medway

river
loose

earthwork

X   ROMAN REMAINS

Ⓧ   SITE OF VILLA

M   MAIDSTONE (POST ROMAN SITE)

Sketch map showing the distribution of Roman and Anglo
Saxon remains in the Maidstone area.

ABOVE: Group of stones known as the Coldrum near
Trottiscliffe, and CENTRE: the Chestnuts at Addington.
LEFT and RIGHT: Roman glass from the Maidstone area,
part of a collection in Maidstone Museum. (MM) BELOW:
Looking towards the complex of buildings which mark the
site of early Maidstone.

ABOVE: The Battle of Aylesford. A detail of the tapestry which hangs in Maidstone Town Hall, depicting the death of Horsa. (MM) BELOW: Aylesford at the turn of the century.

23

ABOVE: Gundolf's Tower at West Malling. Named after
the Bishop of Rochester who founded the Abbey in 1090.
BELOW: West Malling Abbey when it was no longer a
religious institution. A 1773 print.

Prayer and Rebellion

The earliest religious house in the Maidstone area was founded at West Malling. In 1090 Bishop Gundolf of Rochester instituted the building of a Benedictine Abbey on his manor of Malling. Later he gave the land to the nuns of St Mary's Abbey.

In 1119 the Priory of St Mary and St Nicholas for Augustinian canons was founded by Robert de Crepido Corde, or Crevequer, on his land at Leeds. He endowed it with the churches that stood on his extensive estate. By the end of the 13th century Leeds had become crown property, and was to receive endowments from Edward I, so that a daily service would be held for the soul of his late queen consort, Eleanor, in the Chapel of nearby Leeds Castle. Edward II and Edward III gave grants of land to the Priory.

In 1146 William of Ypres, the Earl of Kent gave his manor of Boxley to a French order of Cistercian monks. Here the Abbey of St Mary, its simple style of architecture reflecting the austere rules of the order, was built. Its Abbots were of some importance. In 1171 the Abbot of Boxley helped to hastily bury the murdered Archbishop, Thomas à Becket, and in 1193 the then Abbot of Boxley, with the Abbot of Robertsbridge found the captured Richard I in Bavaria.

In 1240 Richard de Grey, Lord Cudnor returned from the sixth Crusade accompanied by two religious houses of the Carmelites or White Friars from Mount Carmel. The Bishop of Rochester gave his permission for a religious house to be founded on Lord Cudnor's manor at Aylesford. The building of the first Carmelite house in England started. As Lord Cudnor did not have the funds to complete the project the Church granted penance to those who helped in the Priory's construction. In 1247 a meeting of the heads of Carmelite houses of Europe was held at Aylesford. The then Prior General, Alan of Brittany resigned, and Simon (or Simeon) Stock was elected. The new Prior General had joined the order after spending 20 years living in the stump or 'stock' of an oak tree. He was to die a centenarian in 1265, and was buried at Bordeaux, and was to be later cannonised for his Godly life. His bones were brought to Aylesford soon after the Second World War.

Castles were constructed by the Norman landowners, often within sight of the religious houses. These strongholds were built to protect the main routes of communication, demonstrate the power of the new aristocracy, and to act as forts in case of attack. Simple motte and bailey buildings were to be seen at Allington, Leybourne, Thurnham, and perhaps at Leeds. Later stone castles were built at Sutton Valence and West Malling, and were also to replace the wooden buildings of Allington and Leeds.

In the centre of this secular and religious building activity stood Maidstone. The settlement was grouped around the church of St Mary's, which stood above the flood level of the rivers Medway and Len. The Archbishop's manor was little more than a prosperous farming community, the profits of which belonged to the See of Canterbury. It was not until the 1200s that Maidstone became of ecclesiastical importance. In 1186 a disagreement over land ownership had arisen between the monks of Christchurch,Canterbury, and the Archbishop of Canterbury. The argument continued, and in 1193 it was proposed that a rival foundation be established at Maidstone, but as a settlement was reached, Maidstone remained unaltered.

By 1205 the rector of St Mary's Maidstone was the wealthy William Cornhill, but on being enthroned Bishop of Coventry and Litchfield in 1215 he gave his Maidstone home to the archbishop elect, Cardinal Stephen Langton. The Norman building to the south of the present Archbishop's Palace could have been part of this house.

The first Archbishop to show an interest in Maidstone was Boniface, who in c1260 founded a hospice 'Le Newark de Maydestone'. Dedicated to St Peter and St Paul it was run by a master, and housed ten poor persons. It was probably a bridge chapel with hospice attached for travellers.

After the Battle of Hastings, Leeds Castle became the property of Hamon de Crevrecoeur, who had fought beside his cousin William the Conquerer. In 1119 his descendant, Robert, built a stone castle on the site of an earlier fort which stood on an island formed by the river Len. In 1265 Roger de Leybourne, Custodian of the Tower of London, was given Leeds Castle, yet it is also recorded that the Crevecoeur family retained it until 1272. Certainly by 1278 it had become Crown property, and the then reigning Edward I gave it to his wife· Eleanor of Castile.From this time the Castle was traditionally the Queen's Castle, to house the Royal families of succeeding generations. In 1318 the custodianship of Leeds was given to one Bartholomew de Baddlesmere. Little is known of him, other than that he was a rebel. In October 1321 Queen Isabella found her castle locked against her. Her husband, Edward II then arrived from London with a force of its citizens. They besieged the castle, took it, and hung Walter Culpeper, the Governor of the Castle, from its battlements. The siege had repercussions: Edward granted compensation to the monks of Leeds Priory for damage sustained during the action. At Malling Abbey the nuns demanded the removal of the Abbess who was Baddlesmere's sister. Lord Baddlesmere was captured the following year at Boroughbridges, and was executed, his head displayed at Canterbury.

In 1348 John de Ufford, Archbishop elect, died of the Black Death (unconsecrated) on 20 May 1349. In July Thomas Bradwardine was made Archbishop only to die of the plague in August, and in turn was succeeded by Archbishop Simon Islip. Islip sued Ufford's administrator for delapidations of the Palace at Maidstone, and received £1,100 compensation. Stone from the ruined Archbishop's Palace at Wrotham was used to rebuild the Palace at Maidstone, in which Islip was to die, later the same year.

The effect of the Black Death on the population of Maidstone is unrecorded, but it was probably severe as it killed 30% of the population of England. At nearby Malling Abbey the devastation was recorded. Abbess Isabel Packham died of the plague in May 1349. Benedicata de Grey was elected Abbess but died the same evening. Another Abbess was elected only to die three weeks later, and by the end of the visitation the community was reduced to nine.

The Black Death resulted in shortages and inflation. The landowners grazed sheep on the land of those that had died, which meant that they did not have to evict tenants, and gained wealth from wool which was much in demand. The peasants found themselves even poorer, especially when they had to pay a tax to support a failing campaign in France. In 1351 a Statute of Labourers fixed wages and the price of food. The problem came to a head in 1381.

Tradition says that the rebellion was sparked off by a Poll Tax collector at Dartford. He refused to believe that the daughter of a tiler was younger than 15, the age above which the tax was levied. The angry father struck the tax gatherer dead. Certainly on 2 June Lesnes Abbey was attacked, and peasants rose in rebellion in the Home Counties and East Anglia. On 5 June the men of Dartford marched to Rochester, taking the town and releasing prisoners. By 7 June the mob had reached Penenden Heath, where they elected Wat Tyler to lead them. Whether this was the tiler from Dartford, or a resident of Maidstone is uncertain. The rebels marched to Canterbury which they took on the 9th, burning records, releasing prisoners and sacking the castle. They returned to Maidstone on the 11th, where they killed livestock and probably destroyed the manorial rolls which showed for whom the peasants had to work. They broke into the Archbishop's Prison and released John Ball who was serving his third ecclesiastical imprisonment. He joined the rebels' cause, once more having a chance to preach the ideas of John Wycliffe: the Church would be better without the Pope and Archbishops, English rather than Latin should be used in churches; Ball also encouraged the people not to pay tithes to unworthy clergy. At Blackheath on 12 June he preached a sermon on the rhyme: 'When Adam delve and Eve span, Who then was the gentleman?'

The rising took the rich by surprise, and the peasants arrived at London to find the gates open. They sacked Lambeth Palace and broke open the Fleet Prison. On 14 June they met the young Richard II, demanding the abolition of the Poll Tax and the Statute of Labourers which forced them to take any job offered, however small the pay. They called for the abolition of serfdom and outlawry, free use of the forests, only one bishop, the division of Church property among the people, and the choice to pay tithes in money. Richard agreed to these demands, although his advisors had no intention of carrying them out. Perhaps, realising this, the Kentish section of the rebellion stormed the Tower of London, the only people ever to have succeeded. They beheaded Archbishop Sudbury, who as Chancellor they held responsible for their plight.

The next day Wat Tyler again met the King, but was later stabbed by the Mayor of London. As no other leader came forward, Richard II offered his leadership. The mob drifted away, and the rebellion ended. Tyler was dead and John Ball beheaded. Their concessions withdrawn, the peasants returned home to subjection.

In place of Sudbury, Archbishop Courtenay was enthroned. He had plans to enlarge the church at Maidstone. In 1395 Pope Boniface IX authorising its building, and on 2 August Richard II, while staying at nearby Leeds Castle, gave permission to rebuild the church and add a college of a master and 24 chaplains and clerks. This was the time of great cathedral building and Courtenay had two great master masons or architects to choose from: William Wynford, the designer of Winchester Cathedral or Henry Yevele, who was rebuilding the Norman cathedral at Canterbury. As Courtenay's main residence was at Canterbury, he chose Yevele.

The present church of All Saints stands as a fine example of the English Perpendicular style, which has not been radically altered or enlarged. It was completed in three years, and has an overall unity of appearance, as it was designed by just one mason. The stone used was Kentish rag, obtained from local quarries, while the door and window casing are of Caen stone. Stone from the first church was used in the west wall, and one of the original window frames was built into the north wall, (third from the east). Inside, the pillars on the south side of the nave stand on submerged oval plinths, which probably mark the site of the original pillars.

In the church today we can see the original choir stalls with misericords, decorated with arms including those of the last rector of St Mary's, Guido de Mono, Archbishop Courtenay and the arms of his brother. The sixth from the altar on the north side shows an amusing caricature of the college cook.

Part of the ornately carved screen between the north chapel and the chancel came from the hospice of St Peter and St Paul which was incorporated into the College, although keeping its independence.

The College buildings consisted of a gatehouse, refectory, kitchen and scullery, with a dormitory and infirmary above. The tower at the west end of the building is known as the Treasurer's Tower as it housed valuable church plate and documents. Bread and alms were distributed from the bakehouse door just inside the covered gateway.

The Master's House retains much of its original charm. An earlier building stood on the site, proved by a pair of windows on the river side of the house which date to 1300. Much of the west side of the building dates from 1350, whereas the rest of the College was built in 1395.

The complex of buildings was large. The southern gateway still stands at the junction of College Road and College Avenue. Until

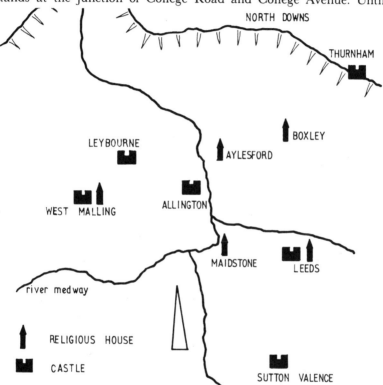

Sketch map showing the position of castles and religious houses in the Maidstone area.

modern times the road ran through this gateway, and the College Gatehouse, to leave by the northern gatehouse, which may also have incorporated a watermill.

A bridge over the Medway, (replaced in 1897), and bridges over the Len at the bottom of Gabriel's Hill, and Bishop's Way, were probably also built at this time.

Courtenay enlarged the Archbishop's Palace, and built the tithe barn, now the Tyrwitt-Drake Museum of Carriages. Only the upper storey of the barn would have been used as such, the ground floor being stables. In the fifteenth century alterations were made: a fireplace was put in the north end of the building, and an unusual outside stairway was added. The upper floor would have been used to house ostlers and the retinue of visitors to the college and manor house, as well as tithes.

The cost of all these buildings was so great that Courtenay obtained a licence from the Pope to tax all the clergy in England by four pence in the pound. The Bishop of Lincoln refused to make the collection in his diocese and appealed to the Pope. Archbishop Courtenay died from fever on 31 July 1396, while the appeal was pending.

Courtenay had originally asked to be buried with his ancestors in Exeter Cathedral, but on his death bed he asked to be laid to rest in the churchyard of Maidstone, saying that he was not fit to be buried inside a church let alone a cathedral. The monks of Canterbury, perhaps remembering the profits brought by the canonisation of Archbishop Thomas à Becket, who lay at Canterbury Cathedral, took Courtenay's body from Maidstone to that city, where he was placed in his official tomb. A brass effigy of Courtenay once had pride of place in the chancel of Maidstone, and tradition said that Courtenay was really buried in All Saints . In 1794 the tomb thought to be Courtenay's was opened, but although it held a skeleton, there was no proof that it was that of the Archbishop.

Courtenay gave something other than the Collegiate buildings to Maidstone: his family arms. The arms were originally those of Geoffrey de Bouillon, a famed warrior of the First Crusade. A Courtenay married a kinswoman of de Bouillon and was allowed to carry the same arms: or three torteaux; on a label azure, three mitres of a field. These were officially incorporated in the official Maidstone arms during the Herald's Visitation of 1619.

The buildings at Maidstone were completed during the time of Archbishop Thomas Arundel. In the year of his enthronement he was banished by Richard II, but in 1399 was able to help his first cousin, Henry Bolingbroke to take the throne. Richard had been on an expedition to Ireland and on his return was met by the usurper. Richard sent for his nephew, Thomas Holland, the Earl of Kent, to make a treaty with Bolingbroke. Holland found himself in the Tower of London and the deposed king was taken to Leeds Castle, tradition says disguised as a forester. It was ironic that Richard should begin his imprisonment in one of his favourite residences. In 1406 Henry IV stayed in Leeds Castle to avoid the plague that was prevalent in London, although by 1419 it had once more become a prison, this time for Henry's Queen, Joan of Navarre.

In 1398 the first Master of the College at Maidstone was appointed; Sir John Wotton. The grand monument above his tomb, near the south-east entrance of All Saints Church, is a record of his personal wealth and status.

In 1414 Archbishop Chicheley, founder of All Souls College Oxford, was enthroned. The young Henry VI stayed at Maidstone as Chicheley's guest in 1437 and a few years later in 1441 the King was to grant a letter patent for a new religious foundation in Maidstone.

The Corpus Christi Fraternity or Guild was a brotherhood of tradesmen and prominent citizens who wished to uphold the doctrine of the Real Presence, hold religious services and relieve sickness. Their Brotherhood Hall was given in 1422 by John Hyssenden 'a noble and venerable man', so the guild had been founded for some years before its confirmation. The hall would have been the centre of business in mediaeval Maidstone. It was staffed by two wardens, four chaplains and a number of churchmen, gentry and townsmen. It consisted of a hall, refectory, a chapel and three cloisters. The Brotherhood also had the use of the chantry chapel in the north chancel of All Saints Church. Each member of the brotherhood gave an annual contribution, varying in size according to means. Membership included the Prior of Leeds, the Abbot of Boxley Abbey, and the Master of All Saints College. The number of members varied between 100 and 200 although the number of sisters rarely rose above 20, in part due to the fact that few women had their own income.

In 1441 Henry VI imprisoned his sister-in-law, Eleanor, Duchess of Gloucester, in Leeds Castle after she was found guilty of witchcraft, heresy, treason and necromancy against the King.

In 1443 Archbishop Chicheley, now 82, asked to be allowed to resign but, before a decision was announced, he died at Maidstone on 12 April 1443. His successor, Archbishop John Stafford, resorted to Maidstone for the benefit of his health. He died there on 25 May 1452. He was followed in September by Cardinal John Kemp, who founded a college similar to the one at Maidstone, at his birth place of Wye near Ashford. He died two years later, being followed by Archbishop Thomas Bourchier, whose badge of an unusual open knot may be seen above a fireplace in the Weavers House, St Faith's Street.

The May of 1450 brought unrest to the people of England. A Kentish rebellion began at Ashford, led by Jack Cade, who claimed to be an illegitimate relation of the Duke of York and who has also been described as an Irish adventurer. He assembled his men on Penenden Heath, many of whom had been called to join the rebellion by the Constables of the Hundreds. Followers included John Miller and Thomas Hall of Hollingbourne, Richard Culpeper of East Farleigh, and William Beale, John Fisher, Robert East, Richard Dyne and John Chamberlain or Smethcote of Maidstone, as well as a mason, waxchandler, goldsmith, tailor and draper from the same town. By July the force reached London with their complaints against the King's administration, which had imposed heavy taxation. They entered London and tried the Treasurer, whom they then executed. After this the citizens and magistrates rose and the rebellion quickly dispersed under a treaty of pardon. Cade was pursued and killed. Maidstone was one of the towns to be pardoned for its part in the rebellion.

Some of the Lancastrians claimed that this was an indication of a Yorkist rebellion, although the Wars of the Roses were not to break out until 1455.

In 1461 Edward of York, supported by some bowmen of Kent and his followers, was victorious at the battle of Towton over Henry VI. Three years later Edward IV married Elizabeth Woodville of Maidstone. The Woodville family came from Grafton in Northamptonshire to live at the Mote, Maidstone in 1369-1370. The Mote had previously been owned by Roger de Leybourne in the 13th century, John de Shoford in the reign of Edward II, and Bartholomew de Burgersh, one of the original knights-companions, during the reign of Edward III. The Woodvilles quickly rose to favour at Court. Richard Woodville became a trusted servant of Henry V, and a friend to the King's brother and Regent in France, the Duke of Bedford. In 1436 Woodville married Jacquetta of Luxembourg, widow of Bedford. The Woodvilles remained close to the Crown, and in 1450 Richard helped to suppress Cade's rebellion. In 1464 Edward IV married Elizabeth, widow of Sir John Grey, a Lancastrian killed at the second Battle of St Albans, and eldest daughter of Richard Woodville. The marriage remained secret for five months.

The year following the coronation of Elizabeth Woodville, five of her sisters were married to some of the greatest in the land, leaving only two bachelor dukes. A scandal arose from the marriage of her 21-year-old brother to the Dowager Duchess of Norfolk who was 70,while her brother Lionel was to become Bishop of Salisbury Cathedral. Her father was created Earl Rivers and Treasurer for England.

Warwick the Kingmaker felt that his support of Edward IV had been to no avail and that the Woodvilles had too much power. As Warden of the Cinque Ports and Keeper of Dover and Sandwich Castles he had a moderate Kentish following. In 1468 (1 January or 25 March,) some of his men raided the Woodvilles' home at Maidstone. By 1469 both the deposed Henry VI and the reigning Edward IV were Warwick's prisoners. Earl Rivers was beheaded at Kenilworth and his remains are now buried in All Saints Church, Maidstone. Warwick restored Henry VI to the throne, and Anthony Woodville fled with Edward to Burgundy. Edward returned the following year to fight at Tewkesbury while Anthony Woodville held London for his friend.

After Edward's resumption of the throne Anthony Woodville, tired of fighting, left England with his wife to make a pilgrimage to St James of Compostella in the autumn of 1471. A friend lent him a French translation of the Latin book *Dictes and Sayings of the Philosophers* and 'finding it a glorious fair mirror to all good Christian people to behold and understand' he translated it into English. This was to become the first book printed in English, and was published by Caxton in 1477.

Woodville became a patron of Caxton who in 1479 published Earl Rivers' devotional book *The Last Four Things*.

In 1473 Lord Rivers was made guardian of his nephew, the Prince of Wales. When, ten years later, Edward IV died in April 1487, Woodville set out with the young Edward for London. They were intercepted by the Dukes of Buckingham and Gloucester, who feared that Lord Rivers might take the throne for himself. Elizabeth Woodville was equally fearful, and took sanctuary with her other children in Westminster. But she had to hand her other son to Gloucester. Lord Rivers was imprisoned in the Tower and the two Princes were placed there for safety.

Neither side trusted the other and various plots were laid. On 25 June Parliament declared that the late Edward IV's marriage to Elizabeth Woodville was invalid and that the children were therefore illegitimate. Richard had some conspirators, including Anthony Woodville, executed. On 6 July the Duke of Gloucester was crowned.

The Duke of Buckingham (who was married to Elizabeth Woodville's sister Katherine), and his first cousin, Henry Earl of Richmond, hatched a plan to depose the King. The rallying point of this rebellion was to be Maidstone where on 18 October the uprising would break out. On 10 October news broke that the Princes had been murdered in the Tower of London and Richard raised an army by 12 October.

The planned rebellion began at Maidstone, led by Sir George Brown of Becheworth, who had been sheriff of Kent in 1481, and was married to Elizabeth Paston. On 18 October some 5,000 men gathered, on 20 October they reached Rochester and by 22 October, Gravesend. Other areas joined in, Guildford rose in support on 25 October, but the western division led by Buckingham was unable to link up due to exceptionally bad weather. The rebel Duke was soon betrayed and beheaded. Henry, Duke of Richmond, and Sir Edward Woodville had sailed from Brittany, but Henry was driven back to France by the storms. The rebellion achieved little, although the Sussex force managed to hold Bodiam Castle until mid-November.

In January 1484 Richard III offered £100 or ten marks of land for the capture of some influential Kentish rebels, and Parliament passed an Act of Attainder, which convicted the conspirators of high treason and confiscated their lands. However, only Sir John Guildford was imprisoned and the majority received pardons.

Several of the rebels, such as Edward and Richard Woodville, had managed to flee England. In 1485 they returned with the Duke of Richmond. The Wars of the Roses were finally ended at the Battle of Bosworth, where Richard III was killed. Richmond became Henry VII and married Elizabeth, the daughter of Edward IV and Elizabeth Woodville of Maidstone.

ABOVE: Leeds Castle, a 19th century view by Shepherd.
BELOW: The Gatehouse at Leeds Castle.

34

ABOVE: Allington Castle. CENTRE: Leybourne Castle.
(KCL) BELOW: St Mary and All Saints College,
Maidstone.

35

ABOVE: The interior of All Saints Church at the beginning of this century. BELOW: The 1381 Peasants' Revolt did not reach a happy conclusion. This engraving depicts Wat Tyler about to be killed, while King Richard rides towards the band of rebels.

An engraving of Jack Cade (leader of the Kentish Rebellion of 1450) in Cannon Street – declaring himself Lord of the City of London.

ABOVE: The misericord of the college cook in All Saints Church. BELOW: The Master's House for the secular college still retains much charm, though its interior was no doubt far more stark in the days of the famous master William Grocyn.

The College Gatehouse had a kitchen and refectory downstairs with a dormitory above. The Treasurer's Tower at the west end was so called because it held church valuables and important documents.

ABOVE: The southern gateway to the college still stands, although the traffic entering Maidstone from the south no longer passes through its impressive archway. BELOW: The Master's House (right of picture).

40

ABOVE: This is all that remains of the northern gatehouse. Because it backs onto the River Len it is possible that it was a watermill at some time. CENTRE: Under the present bridge which crosses the River Len there is a much older bridge which was probably built at the same time as the Archbishop's Palace. BELOW: The Tythe Barn, another important building of the college complex. Seen here at the beginning of this century.

ABOVE: The Tythe Barn or Archbishop's Stables as seen today, after restoration. LEFT: This statue of Archbishop Courtenay can still be seen on the front of this Victorian building in Bank Street. RIGHT: The tomb of John Wotton, the first master of the college.

ABOVE: This painting on the back of John Wotton's tomb shows Wotton being presented to the Virgin Mary by the saints. BELOW: This painting of the interior of All Saints Church made during the last century shows the sedilia. (MM)

ABOVE: This house known as the Weavers contains a fire place above which are the arms of Archbishop Thomas Bourchier. LEFT: William Caxton, who published the first book printed in English in 1477, *The Dictes and Sayings of the Philosophers*. It was translated into English by Anthony Woodville of Maidstone who was to become the printer's patron. RIGHT: Elizabeth Woodville, who was born in Maidstone, married Edward IV in 1464. Her two sons were murdered in the Tower of London in 1487.

44

Royal Flush

In 1486 John Morton, a supporter of the Buckingham Rebellion, was enthroned as Archbishop of Canterbury. He took an interest in his manor at Maidstone. He had the Palace repaired and enlarged, probably using the proceeds of his taxation known as Morton's Fork: if you lived simply then you could afford to hand over your savings, and if you lived extravagantly then you should spend less on yourself, and give it to his friend King Henry VII.

Archbishop Henry Dean succeeded Morton in 1501, to be quickly followed in 1503 by Archbishop William Warham. Warham carried out further work on the Palace at Maidstone; his arms of a goat and three scallop shells and the arms of the See of Canterbury can be seen over several fireplaces in the Palace.

It was Warham, who in 1506 presented the Mastership of the Collegiate Church of All Hallows, Maidstone, to his old tutor, William Grocyn. Grocyn was a pioneer in the translation of Greek literature into English, and was one of the first publicly to teach Greek at Oxford University. He was a friend of many figures of the Renaissance: the Italian printer Aldus Manutius, the painter Holbein whom he brought to England, and the Dutch theologian Erasmus who was for a while the rector of the church at Aldington near Lympne.

On the death of Henry VII in 1509, his son acceded to the throne. The young Henry VIII was to encourage an artistic renaissance and a religious reformation. He turned Leeds Castle into a grand palace, adding an upper storey to the gloriette, and building a tower for the Maids of Honour. It has been suggested that on his way to the Cloth of Gold in 1520 he stayed at Leeds Castle and on his return journey, at the Archbishop's Palace at Maidstone.

In 1531 Henry VIII was acknowledged to be the Head of the Church of England. This action was taken after the Pope had refused the King a divorce: Henry quickly appreciated the financial potential and scrutinised the wealth of the religious houses. Many objected and in 1535 Elizabeth Rede, the Abbess of Malling Abbey refused to admit Sir Thomas Wyatt, who planned to confiscate the Abbey. It was eventually closed 29 October 1537. Boxley Abbey was dissolved on 29 January 1538. Its holy rood of a crucified Christ which 'miraculously' moved its eyes, and spoke, was taken to Maidstone on market day, where its ingenious workings were displayed. It was then taken to

London where it was burnt outside St Paul's. On 30 July 1538 Aylesford Priory was dissolved. Leeds Priory was not dissolved until 18 March 1540. The lands were transferred to the Crown, and the possessions were sold to provide for the nuns and monks. The Abbot of Boxley received £50, the Prioress of Malling £40 and the Prior of Leeds £80, while monks received a pension of £4 a year and nuns £2.

The properties of Boxley and Aylesford were sold to Sir Thomas Wyatt of Allington, while the land of Leeds Priory was acquired by the Dean and Chapter of Rochester, the actual buildings being sold to Anthony St Leger, the Lord Deputy of Ireland when he was granted Leeds Castle by the young Edward VI in 1550. Leeds Priory buildings were eventually taken down in 1790. The Priory at Malling became the property of the Archbishop of Canterbury, and was not used for a religious purpose until it was bought by Mrs Charlotte Boyd for Anglican nuns in 1892.

The College of Priests was not dissolved until 1546, and three years later it was bought by George Brooke, Lord Cobham. The buildings gradually fell into disuse. The last remaining part of the Hospice of St Peter and St Paul was at one time used as a brewery store. In 1836 a curate of All Saints Church, Rev F.F. Haslewood took an interest in the building. It was restored in 1837 by the architect John Whichcord, and by 1840 had its own parish.

The Fraternity of Corpus Christi was dissolved in 1547. The Hall was bought by the town with the proceeds of the church plate of All Saints, and used as a grammar school.

The Archbishop's Palace was not affected by the dissolution, having been exchanged by Archbishop Cranmer in 1537 for various lands belonging to Henry VIII. The King granted the building to Sir Thomas Wyatt. Victorian historians give the date as 14 June 1540, though the dates 1546, and 13 June 1550 have also been given. Certainly Edward VI gave it to Sir Thomas Wyatt jnr to be held in knight's service, on the latter date.

The year before Henry VIII's accession to the throne Sir Henry Wyatt was appointed his guardian. Just as the Woodvilles had become close to the house of York, the Wyatts became involved with the Tudors.

Sir Henry Wyatt bought Allington Castle in 1492, and it was here, in the picturesque curve of the river Medway, that the Wyatt family were to make their home for the next 60 years. The first recorded holder of the manor of Allington was Ulnoth, the younger brother of King Harold. After the Norman Conquest it was held by King William's half brother Odo, followed by William de Warrene and Osbert de Longchamp. A wooden fort was built on the site during the reign of Richard II, but was destroyed on the orders of Henry II. The site was not rebuilt until Sir Stephen de Pencestre, Warden of the Cinque Ports obtained a licence in 1282 to build a small stone castle. On Pencestre's death the property passed to his daughter's husband, who was a member of the Cobham family. It remained Cobham property until the time of Edward IV when it went to the Brent family, from whom the Wyatts bought the castle, which they improved and enlarged.

Sir Henry Wyatt had been held by Richard III in the Tower for two years, because of his Yorkist sympathies. Family tradition relates that he was kept alive by a cat who brought him pigeons. He was released on the accession of Henry VII, of whom he quickly became a trusted friend. In 1508 the King made him a Privy Councillor and guardian of his son.

Sir Henry Wyatt's son was born at Allington Castle on 24 February 1503. Thomas was to gain considerable fame as a poet, and for his introduction of the sonnet from Italy. As a young man he formed a close friendship with Anne, daughter of Sir Thomas Boleyn, with whom Sir Henry Wyatt was Joint Constable of Norwich Castle. Thomas continued his relationship with Anne, even after his marriage to Elizabeth Brooke, the daughter of Lord Cobham. When in 1526 Henry VIII fell in love with Anne Boleyn, Thomas warned the King of her, and confessed his friendship. This candid approach gained Henry VIII's trust; Thomas was sent on a mission to Rome, which was the start of a distinguished diplomatic career.

In 1527 Henry VIII stayed at Allington Castle on his way to meet Cardinal Wolsey, who was then trying to gain the King's divorce from Catherine of Aragon. The attempt failed. Henry made himself head of the English Church and married Anne in 1533. Thomas Wyatt, now a Privy Councillor, acted in his father's place as ewer bearer at Anne's coronation.

Three years later, as Anne had not produced a son, Henry VIII wished to marry Jane Seymour. Anne Boleyn was committed to the Tower of London on suspicion of adultery. On 5 May 1536 Thomas Wyatt was also put in the Tower, where he revealed the facts of his affair with Anne. This helped her downfall, but allowed the Wyatts to remain in Royal favour. On 19 May 1536 Anne, attended by Thomas's sister, was executed.

On 13 February 1542 another of Henry's wives was to suffer a similar fate. Catherine Howard could have been brought up in the home of her maternal cousins, the Culpepers of Greenway Court Hollingbourne. She became closely attached to her cousin Thomas and when Lord Howard remarried, Catherine went to live with her stepmother in London. Here Catherine attracted the King's attention and he appointed her lady-in-waiting to Anne of Cleves. Thomas Culpeper was made a body attendant to Henry VIII, and the two men became great friends. The King divorced Anne of Cleves, and on 28 July 1540, married the 21-year-old Catherine. In the Autumn of 1541 enemies conferred against the new Queen, and Archbishop Cranmer passed a note to the King. Catherine was taken from Hampton Court to Syon

House, and Thomas Culpeper was taken to the Tower of London. Thomas insisted even under torture that Catherine was innocent but on 10 December 1540 was executed on Tyburn. Catherine was taken to the Tower, where she insisted that she had remained faithful to Henry after their marriage. She was condemned to death without trial, and on 13 February 1542, was executed on the same spot as that other Kentish Queen, Anne Boleyn. Catherine Howard's last words were 'I die a Queen, but I would rather die the wife of a Culpeper'.

On 14 June 1536 Thomas Wyatt was released from the Tower, and to demonstrate his continuing loyalty to the King, fought against Lincolnshire rebels. The following May, he was made High Sheriff of Kent and knighted. In April 1538 he was again arrested, this time on a false charge of treason. Although soon released, his name was not finally cleared until 1540.

When Sir Thomas Wyatt died in October 1542 his young son, also Thomas, was forced to sell outlying estates to pay debts. The young Wyatt lacked his father's diplomacy. In 1543, with his friend Henry Howard, the Earl of Surrey, he was put in the Tower of London for rabble-rousing during Lent. They were quickly released and Wyatt distinguished himself as a soldier in the French campaign. The young Edward IV made Wyatt a Sheriff of Kent, and it may have been at this time, June 1550, that he was granted the old Archbishop's Palace of Maidstone.

In 1553 Lady Jane Grey was to hold the throne for nine days. Sir Thomas Wyatt conspired against her father-in-law, who had pressed her claim to the Crown. Mary I quickly came to the throne, and made moves to re-establish the Church of Rome. The Wyatts, themselves Roman Catholics, were in sympathy with this move. Queen Mary, wishing to become closer to her maternal home, announced on 15 January 1554, that she was to marry Prince Philip of Spain.

Many feared that the Queen's marriage would make England an annexe of Spain. Edward Courtenay, the Earl of Devonshire persuaded Thomas Wyatt to join him in insurrection against the marriage. Wyatt agreed and managed to get a vague promise of help from the French ambassador.

On 23 January 1554 Anthony Norton of Trottiscliffe, Robert Rudstone of Boughton Monchelsea, Alexander Fisher and 'another gentleman' met with Wyatt at Allington Castle. Fisher was asked to get William Tilden, a draper and mayor of Maidstone two years earlier, to persuade the people of Maidstone to join the cause, and march to London.

On the evening of 24 January Wyatt sent a message to the Sheriff of Kent, Sir Robert Southwell (who lived at Mereworth and was reputed to be against the planned marriage), asking him and Lord Abergavenny to join the rising. A verbal reply, denouncing Wyatt as a traitor, was sent to Allington, the messenger remaining with the Sheriff.

The next morning Sir Thomas Wyatt, Sir Henry Isley of Vinters, and George Maplesden of Digons (a house which once stood on the south side of Knightrider Street,) and Sir Thomas Isley of Boxley rode into Maidstone. Here a proclamation signed by Wyatt, George Harper of Sutton Valence, Sir Henry Isley and several others, was read out denouncing the marriage, saying that Spaniards had landed at Dover, and were already at Rochester. Sir Thomas Wyatt stressed he had no wish to harm the Queen with whom he had no quarrel.

The men rallied on Penenden Heath. Wyatt left with a force of 1,500, encouraged by promises of a further 5,000. On 26 January they took Rochester and cannon were smuggled in from London.

The following day, Lord Abergavenny met Sir Robert Southwell at Malling. Here a proclamation was read offering pardon to all those who had joined Wyatt. Just after midnight on the 28th Sir Henry Isley, with some 500 men on their way from the Weald via Sevenoaks to Rochester, was spotted by the opposing force. The news reached Malling, and Southwell wrote to the Privy Council asking the Lord Warden of the Cinque Ports and other gentlemen to go with their men to Rochester. Then Southwell, with Lord Abergavenny and some 600 men, left West Malling. They intercepted Isley and his force near Wrotham Heath. On Blacksole Field the insurgents fled, Abergavenny's force taking 60 prisoners.

Realising the seriousness of the situation at last, the Queen sent the Duke of Norfolk with some 600 men to Gravesend. From here a messenger was sent to Rochester with the offer of pardon, earlier announced at Malling. Wyatt stated that he and his men had done nothing wrong and therefore did not need a pardon.

Sir George Harper, one of the leaders of the Wyatt rebellion, rode after the messenger to Gravesend. After asking to be pardoned, he urged the Duke of Norfolk to send troops to prevent Wyatt reaching London.

Wyatt now felt disillusioned: Canterbury had sent no help, and the promised troops had either not materialised or had been prevented from joining. One narrative even states that he was preparing to take flight abroad.

The Duke of Norfolk had fewer men than Wyatt and feared that some were in league with the rebels. He wanted to delay his attack on Rochester until he was joined by the Sheriff, the Lord Warden and East Kent forces. He advanced towards Rochester with an increased force of 700.

At about four o'clock on 29 January the force reached Strood. The octogenarian Duke, veteran of Flodden Field, placed himself at the head of his men and gave the order to disperse the opposition. Then Sir Edward Bray called out that the Londoners were changing sides. Before realising what was happening, Sir George Harper and one Captain Brett came forward. Brett announced that he did not want to fight countrymen who were trying to preserve England from foreign domination and was therefore joining Wyatt. Norfolk quickly retreated with Lord Arundel and a few supporters. Wyatt and his men crossed the river from Medway and joined his new supporters. They claimed Norfolk's baggage and eight cannon.

Lord Abergavenny had assembled a force of 200 at Maidstone. They were marching towards Rochester when news of Norfolk's troops' defection to Wyatt came through. Abergavenny's men then left for their homes or deserted to Wyatt, and Abergavenny was forced to take refuge at Sir Robert Southwell's house at Mereworth.

On 30 January Wyatt led his force to his uncle's home at Cooling Castle. They captured the castle, took Lord Cobham prisoner, and advanced to Dartford.

Wyatt then received a deputation from the Queen who, stalling for time, asked to know Wyatt's demands. He demanded the Tower of London, the Queen, and a change in her councillors.

On the morning of 1 February, Queen Mary addressed the citizens of London at Guildhall and by the next day 20,000 had enrolled in her cause.

On 3 February, £100 in annual perpetuity was offered for the capture of Sir Thomas Wyatt. By now Wyatt and his force had reached Southwark, but had been prevented from crossing London Bridge and had to retreat, many deserting.

Three days later Wyatt managed to cross the Thames and on 7 February, Wyatt, with 24 remaining followers entered the City, to be surrounded at Temple Bar. He submitted and was taken to the Tower. On 15 March he was tried at Westminster and on 11 April beheaded on Tower Hill.

Many of those who took part in the rebellion were caught, especially the gentlemen who had signed the proclamation, or were named in the fighting. Alexander Fisher, William Green, Peter Mapelsden, Richard Parke, William Smythe and William Tilden were held under guard in Allington Castle by the Sheriff of Kent. Poorer prisoners were held in the small Maidstone jail. Sir Henry and Sir Thomas Isley were hanged at Maidstone at the end of February. Anthony and William Knyvett and one Mantell were hanged at Sevenoaks while Captain Brett and several others were hanged at Rochester.

Others were more fortunate. Lord Cobham's two sons and Robert Rudstone were condemned to death but sentence was never carried out. Many, such as William Tilden and John Hall of Maidstone, were pardoned.

Estates of those who took part were confiscated and divided among the Queen's friends. The Wyatts' lands of Allington, Aylesford, Boxley and Maidstone were seized, although Lady Wyatt was allowed to live at Maidstone. It was not until 1570 that Wyatt's son, George, was allowed to own Boxley. High fines were imposed. Peter Maplesden, who lived at Chillington Manor House (now Maidstone Museum and Art Gallery), had to pay £133 6s 8d.

Vinters, home of the Isleys, was granted by Queen Mary to Henry Cutt of Binbury and she granted the Archbishop's Palace to Cardinal Pole.

Altogether some 150 were executed in London and Kent while 303 received the Queen's pardon. The rebellion also caused Maidstone to lose its Town Charter.

In July 1554 Queen Mary married Prince Philip of Spain. It was not a successful match and produced no children. In 1555 the Prince's father abdicated his throne, and so, after only 14 months Philip returned to Spain to become the most powerful person in Europe. Mary died in November 1558.

Queen Elizabeth brought stability to England. She never stayed in Maidstone, even though two of her courtiers lived in the town.

Queen Mary had given Digons, the Maplesdon home, to a lawyer from a Teston family called Nicholas Barham. In 1561 Barham bought Chillington Manor House. (This was also a Mapelsden family property, and Queen Elizabeth restored it to them, following confiscation after the Wyatt rebellion.) He rebuilt part of the Manor House and constructed the central Elizabethan section of the present building. The year following this purchase he became one of the first two members of Parliament for Maidstone, the other being Henry Fisher. Barham grew in Royal favour and in 1572 was in charge of the trial of the Duke of Norfolk accused of high treason for conspiring with the Queen of Scots to depose Queen Elizabeth. Barham used unscrupulous methods such as the rack to gain evidence which resulted in Norfolk's and his secretary's death sentences.

In 1573 Barham became one of the Queen's serjeants. Only four years later, while attending the Oxford assizes, he contracted a serious form of gaol fever. He was one of 500 who died during the five week outbreak.

When Cardinal Pole died in November 1558, Queen Elizabeth granted the Archbishop's Palace at Maidstone to Archbishop Mathew Parker. The Palace later became the property of the Queen's favourite; Robert, Earl of Leicester, who sold it. It is recorded as belonging first to Edward Care, then William Doddington, who in c 1580 sold it to a Privy Councillor named Thomas Astley. On 8 July 1581 Thomas sold it to his brother John for £500, the estate consisting of 'all that capital messuage or chief manion-house commonly called or known by the name of the Old Palace, with appurtenances, in Maydenstone, and the malt house commonly called the Old Palace stable, and the land old stable close, and Palace mead and dovehouse, and the Palace pound and Palace close'.

The first recorded local connection of the Astleys was in 1568, when Queen Elizabeth granted Sir John Astley the old Wyatt lands at

Aylesford, Boxley and Allington. The latter was granted on a lease for 30 years for knight's service and an annual rent of £100 2s 7d. In 1583 he was granted Allington in perpetuity and it was in turn leased to the Best family, who resided there until the death of the last of the Astleys in 1719, when it was bought by Sir Robert Romney.

The Astleys were a Norfolk family but lived mainly in the Old Palace. Sir John was related by his maternal aunt's marriage to the Boleyn family, and thus to the Queen. This tenuous family relationship may be why he served in the young Princess's house. On the accession of Queen Mary, Sir John and his wife, Katherine, left England, not returning until after her death in 1558. He was soon appointed Master of the Jewel House in the Tower of London, while his wife became Chief Gentlewoman of the Privy Chamber. In the Parliaments of 1585 and 1588 he represented Maidstone, but is chiefly remembered for his book published in 1585 *The art of Riding, being By a Gentleman of great skill and long experience in the Art.*

His son, also Sir John, became Master of the Jewel House and Master of the Revels at the court of James I. It was probably during this time that the Jacobean panelling in the main hall of the Old Palace was installed. Here above the fireplace, the Astley arms of a pierced cinquefoil and crest of feathers issuing from a ducal coronet, were carved into the oak, above those of Archbishop Warham. The Astley arms may also be seen on the Jacobean font in All Saints.

On Sir John's death in 1639 without an heir, the property passed to his second cousin, grandson of the previously mentioned Thomas. Sir Jacob Astley fought as a general in the Civil War on the Royalist side. Before the battle of Edgehill he rallied his men with 'Lord, thou knowest how busy I must be this day. If I forget thee do not forget me – March on boys'. He was later to be taken prisoner and spent the remainder of the war living at the Old Palace.

The Maidstone town records of 1595-6 include the entry 'Geven to Mr Washington's man when he boughte halfe a buck ijs vjd'. This was the second son of Lawrence and Amee Washington of Sulgrave Manor,Northamptonshire.Their eldest son Robert was the direct ancestor of America's first President, George Washington.

Lawrence Washington leased an acre of land in Knightrider Street for an annual rent of 26s 8d from 1598. In April 1601 he was admitted to the freedom of the Borough when he was 56. On 9 March 1602 he was chosen with Sir Francis Fane as a member of Parliament for Maidstone. He lived in a house on the east side of Stone Street, called Jordan's Hall, but resided most of his time in Maidstone at his house on the south side of Knightrider Street. In July 1964, despite much concern and unsuccessful fund-raising by British and American conservationists, the house in Knightrider Street where Washington lived, and which was originally part of the College buildings dating back to 1395, was demolished.

In 1619 Lawrence Washington died, and was buried at nearby All Saints. His son erected a monument to his father, which now stands near the south door of the church. The monument includes the family arms of three stars and two stripes, upon which the American flag was to be later based.

Washington is not the only American connection with Maidstone. In July and August of 1618 Gabriel Barber, an agent in the lottery of plantations of Virginia, gave the town a gilt cup intended for communion, and £31 to be used for the poor.

In 1608 Sir Warham Leger sold Leeds Castle and joined the expedition of Sir Walter Raleigh to Guiana up the Or inocoRiver.

The ownership of Leeds Castle then passed from the Culpepers to the Fairfaxes. The 6th Lord Fairfax owned Leeds and 5,200,000 acres in Virginia. In 1746-7 he retired to live on his American estate. His cousin Anne was married to Lawrence Washington, the older brother of George, the first President of the United States of America.

ABOVE: An 18th century print of the grand Archbishop's Palace, and BELOW: as seen early this century.

OPPOSITE ABOVE: The Abbey Gateway and Chapel at West Malling. CENTRE: St Peter's Chapel as drawn 100 years ago for Russell's *History of Maidstone*. LEFT: Sir Thomas Wyatt, poet. (MC) RIGHT: The Dove House at Allington Castle. (KCL) ABOVE: Allington Castle has the appearance of a home rather than a fort, seen here in the 17th century. BELOW: Sir Thomas Wyatt the younger, who led the rebellion which opposed Queen Mary's wish to marry Prince Phillip of Spain. (MC)

ABOVE: Mereworth Castle was built during the 18th century, near the site of the home of Sir Robert Southwell. BELOW: Old houses in King Street, West Malling. It was from West Malling that some 600 men left to intercept part of the Wyatt Rebellion.

ABOVE: Allington Castle, confiscated from the Wyatts after the rebellion. (KCL) BELOW: The now redundant Parish Church of St Laurence at Allington stands close to the Castle. This picture shows it as it was after being rebuilt by the Victorians.

ABOVE: The Museum at Maidstone stands on the site of
the earlier Chillington Manor House which was the home of
Peter Maplesden. BELOW: Allington Castle which became
the property of the influential Astley family.

ABOVE: This early Tudor cottage stands on the corner of St Faiths Street and Station Road. It was built c1485-1500. BELOW: This 15th century timber-framed house, known as Mill Farm House, has a dragon beam on its corner with hundreds of nails in it where public notices have been nailed.

ABOVE: Washington's House in Knightrider Street was for many years the vicarage for all Saints Church. It was demolished in 1964. LEFT: Sir Lawrence Washington. His monument in All Saints Church bears the Washington Arms upon which the American flag was later based. RIGHT: Although this building might look old it was built as recently as the last century. One of the statues is of Sir Lawrence Washington.

In the King's Cause

In 1634 Ship money and Tonnage and Poundage were introduced. The idea was to raise, in the form of a 'loan', money with which to rebuild the navy that James I had neglected. Inland towns were expected to contribute to the cost of equipping a vessel. In 1636 Maidstone was told to produce £160. The town refused and then found itself taxed more. The first amount was small compared with the £8,000 needed for an 800 ton ship. This time the complaint was justified, and the amount reduced to £6,400 for a 640 ton ship. In 1640 the proportion of tax to ship was raised to £100 per 100 tons. Maidstone was severely reprimanded for refusing payment. Parliament agreed with the people, and that year declared Ship money to be 'beyond all cavil' and deprived Charles I of his power to collect the money through parliamentary means.

Religious reforms also added to the unrest. Archbishop Laud attempted to find a liturgy fitting to the period, but it was highly unpopular, and caused several petitions to be raised in Kent.

In February 1642 a small, moderately phrased petition, asking for reforms, was sent from East Kent to Parliament. When the Maidstone Assizes for the Western Division of Kent opened on 22 March the same year, it decided to send Parliament a similar petition, this time supported by a large proportion of the county's gentry. This asked Parliament to come to terms with the King, and enquired whose orders, (Parliament's or the King's) the army was to obey. Many at the assizes feared Parliament would object, and so only 19 signed. Parliament committed the presiding judge of the Assizes, Sir Thomas Mallet, to the Tower for not opposing the petition, and the Mayor of Maidstone, Thomas Stanley was summoned to Westminster, where after one week he had still not been told of the charges against him. On 19 April, at the quarter sessions, an attempt was made to disown the petition, but it continued to gain signatures until 29 April, when it was presented at Westminster by Richard Lovelace. It was not favourably received and Sir Edward Dering of Pluckley, who originally raised the idea and three of those who organised it, Sir Roger Twisden of East Peckham, Sir George Stroode of Westerham and the Hon Richard Spencer of Orpington, were arrested and held in a house in Covent Garden. They were later released on bail.

At the July Maidstone Assizes Sir Thomas Mallet once more

presided. Parliament sent a Committee of 17, including Sir Francis Barham of Boughton Monchelsea and Sir Humphrey Tufton of the Mote, members for Maidstone, apparently to dispense justice, though they had no real power so to do. The Assize justices objected, fearing that their judgements would be invalid, and realising that the Committee was there to prevent any further petitions. The Assizes opened, and on 26 July there were several angry exchanges. That evening the young Royalists of the area met and drew up a protest to be taken to Parliament on behalf of the 'Commons of Kent' by one of the knights of the shire. They included Sir John Mainy of Linton Place, Sir John Tufton of the Mote, Sir Edward Filmer of East Sutton, Sir Anthony St Leger of Weirton, Mr Rycaut of the Friars Aylesford, and William Clark of Wrotham. The petition was given to Augustine Sinner of Tutsham Hall, West Farleigh, to present to Parliament. He was told to say that Kent, unlike the West Country, was peaceful and that they had devised a basis for a settlement between Parliament and King. This envisaged that military supplies would be released to the King, the navy restored to him, the army stood down until legal protection for all English subjects was devised, and that the two opposing sides would meet for discussions.

The same petition was sent to Charles at York by Mainy, Filmer and Clark on 1 August. The King replied on 4 August, saying that a general had been made to command his subjects against him, and assuring the petitioners of his protection.

The petition offended Parliament. Spencer, Twisden and Stroode were taken to London, their estates confiscated until they paid Parliament a large sum of money. Parliament despatched troops to Kent. At the Friars, Aylesford, the Rycault home, they seized arms and plate, some of which was hidden in the roof. Sir Peter Rycault was arrested and sent to Upnor Castle. Sir William Boteler, (or Butler) had his house of Barham Court, Teston searched. The estate was sequestrated and he had to pay over £3,000 for its return. The troops found the shops of Maidstone shut against them and they lodged the night in the town. Only two men caused trouble, and were quickly taken to an improvised gallows, where a pretence reprieve was produced, one man released, and the other joining the army, which left for Canterbury to return to London via Maidstone at the end of August.

The rift between Charles I and Parliament was now beyond reconciliation. The Royal standard was raised at Nottingham, and several Kentish gentry, including Lord Lovelace, who presented the April petition and Sir William Clark of Hollingbourne, joined the King. Sir Jacob Astley, who owned the Old Palace of Maidstone, and Sir John Culpeper of Leeds Castle both became members of the King's Council of War.

Kent remained peaceful during the First Civil War, although during

August the Parliamentarians took Rochester Castle without resistance, similar gains taking place at Dover, Walmer and Sandown Castles. Knowle House, Sevenoaks was siezed, and Rochester and Canterbury cathedral organs smashed.

The tide had now turned in favour of Parliament. On 25 October 1643 Maidstone received a letter ordering trained soldiers and volunteers on horse and foot to assemble on Penenden Heath.

Kent was now governed by a County Committee, which was drawn from the Deputy County Lietenants and justices of the peace. Although the Committee was powerful, it had never been legally constituted. In 1643 it was based at Knowle House, but in 1644 moved to the Friars at Aylesford. By 1646 the Committee was based in the main hostelry, the Star Inn at Maidstone.

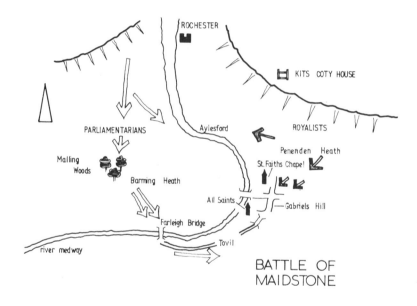

Sketch map showing the battle of Maidstone.

In June 1647 Parliament banned religious festivals. Despite this, the following Christmas Day the people of Canterbury celebrated. Royalists took the city over. This marked the beginning of the second part of the War. Parliament took Canterbury at the end of January 1648, several of those arrested being sent to the commandered Leeds Castle of Royalist Sir John Culpeper. The rebels were tried in May. The carefully chosen jury refused to produce a verdict, finding the charges invalid. They were then told the decision would come from Westminster. The grand jury at Canterbury adopted a petition to the two Houses at Westminster, asking that the forces under Lord Fairfax be demobilised, and stating their loyalty to the King, who was imprisoned in Carisbrooke Castle.

On 16 May the Committee of Kent met at Maidstone. They ordered a supression of the latest petition, and began to muster men for their cause. At Maidstone only 20 men are said to have rallied to the Committee's call. The petition continued to gain signatures.

Edward Hales of Tunstall Green was persuaded to raise some men to take the petition to London. The Royalists met and elected him as their general. Supporters quickly gathered. The Committee of Kent left Maidstone for the Friars at Aylesford, where they were apprehended by the Royalists.

Hales and his men then began their journey to London. At Rochester they were met by two members sent by Parliament, who asked them to go home. The messengers were forcibly held, to Parliament's fury. When the Royalists arrived at Blackheath, Lord Fairfax refused to let them proceed and announced that they would be forgiven if they laid down their arms. The Royalists retreated, and Fairfax, with a Parliamentary force of 7,000, entered the county. This army divided into three, one column to relieve the besieged Dover Castle, and another to Rochester where, finding the town strongly defended, they rejoined the third column led by Lord General Fairfax himself.

On 1 June Fairfax left Meopham, and marched east to be joined at Malling by the Parliamentarians who came via Rochester.

The Royalists assembled on Penenden Heath under the Earl of Norwich. His men numbered 10,000, but many were untrained. Some Parliamentarians were sighted through a 'spyglass'. Norwich sent 1,000 men to Aylesford, and 3,000 to Maidstone. The Parliamentarians were probably those marching from Rochester, for Fairfax had a good idea of the position of the Royalist forces, and did not try to enter Maidstone from the west or north. Instead the army proceeded through East Malling Wood to Barming Heath. Fairfax sent a small party towards Aylesford to appear to be manoeuvering, as the Royalists expected, while the main force turned south, marching past the old Barming rectory, and down to East Farleigh bridge. The bridge was defended by a small group which was easily defeated. The Parliamentary Army then continued to Tovil.

Under the direction of the governor of Maidstone, Sir Gamaliel Dudley, the people of Maidstone spent Thursday 1 June preparing to defend the town. Earthworks were built on the south side of Maidstone, streets were barricaded with trees, and a stockade built across Gabriel's Hill. Cannon were positioned at the cross roads at the top of the High Street, so they could either fire down the High Street to the bridge, or south, down Gabriel's Hill. Royalist troops were positioned by chief lieutenant Sir John Mainy, and Sir William Brockman.

At seven o'clock in the evening, one of the troops posted to the south of Maidstone, rode into the town with news that a Parliamentary force had crossed East Farleigh bridge. The fine weather had suddenly deteriorated into torrential rain. Royalist troops were dispatched to hinder the Parliamentarians, by firing on them from behind hedges. The news of Fairfax's advance, and a request for reinforcements was sent to the Earl of Norwich. Soon 800 men under Colonel Brockman arrived in Maidstone, bringing the Royalist force in Maidstone to 3,000. Brockman and his men were immediately sent towards Tovil, where they fought hand to hand with Parliamentarians, gaining some success. Fairfax, seeing his troops in confusion, alighted from his coach and rallied his men on horseback. The Royalists were driven back, and Fairfax led his troops towards Maidstone.

The Parliamentarians proceeded along 'Tovil Lane' (now called Old Tovil Road), and onto the main road into the town, Stone Street. In the upper part of Stone Street 60 of Fairfax's horsemen met Royalists with a standard. Fierce fighting took place, but gradually the Parliamentary troops gained ground. They passed Knightrider Street, and crossed over the river Len at Little Bridge, (this bridge is covered by the present road) and into the heavily defended Gabriel's Hill. The Royalist cannon were turned on the troops, and they were shot at from the houses on each side of the road.

On hearing of Fairfax's continued advance, General Norwich deliberated on what action to take. When he left Kits Coty for Maidstone, he met opposition, and it was clear that the town was about to fall to Parliament. Norwich turned his men, and marched towards Rochester.

It was after midnight when the last of the Royalists surrendered in St Faith's churchyard. The Victorian historian Russell states that they surrendered in All Saints, but this church is near the low land of the river, while St Faith's stands at the highest point of the town, towards which the action had proceeded. However, there is little doubt that it had been a difficult battle, Parliament winning the town 'by inches'. The Royalists' losses were great: 300 killed, including Sir John Mainy; 1,400 taken prisoner including Sir Gamaliel Dudley and Sir William Brockman; 500 horses, 8 cannon, 3,000 arms, 16 barrels of gun powder, and 12 large barrels of match. Parliamentary forces had lost many men, but were encouraged by their victory. When the news of Maidstone's fall reached Parliament in London, the messenger was paid £10, and a thanksgiving for victory was ordered in the churches of London.

The morning after the battle, Fairfax's men searched the town, finding many weapons in houses. All Saints Church was desecrated.

The Royalists under Norwich left Rochester for Greenwich, where they hoped to meet Royalists from Surrey and Essex. There were no such reinforcements, and many deserted the army, the remainder continuing to Colchester.

On 3 June Fairfax left Maidstone. He marched to Rochester, but on finding the Royalists gone, continued into east Kent. With the taking of Sandown Castle on 5 September, the Kentish rising finally ended.

In November 1648 a parliamentary supporter, Andrew Broughton was elected Mayor of Maidstone. Broughton resided in a house on the south side of Earl Street. He built up a prosperous practice as an attorney, and on 30 January 1630 was admitted a freeman of the borough. In December, 1644 he was made an attorney for the Corporation, defending it in law suits. During his mayoralty he sold a small mace and with other money bought a Commonwealth-style mace. Broughton had become a clerk of the High Court of Justice, and in this capacity was in attendance at the trial of Charles I in January 1649. On the eighth day of the trial, the sentence of death was read by him. On returning to Maidstone, Broughton was attacked in a sermon by the incumbent Wilson. On the phrase: 'David's heart smote him when he cut off the skirt of Saul's garment, but men dare nowadays to cut off the head of a king without remorse', Broughton rose from his seat. Wilson continued: 'When the word of God comes home to a man, it makes him gly for it'. It is said that Broughton never again attended services at All Saints Church. On 30 January Charles I was beheaded and it was a Maidstone surgeon, Thomas Trapham, who embalmed the monarch's body.

At the end of Broughton's term as mayor, he remained a jurat, and represented the town at the Commonwealth parliament. In November 1559 Broughton was elected mayor for a second term, Gervase Maplesden holding the position in his absence.

It is perhaps ironic that General Fairfax, who had won such a sound victory at Maidstone for the Parliamentarians was in 1660 sent to bring Charles II from the Hague to be King of England.

On 5 June it is recorded that representatives of the council were sent to Broughton's house in Earl Street, to ask why he had not attended council meetings. The servants of the house did not know the whereabouts of Broughton. On 6 June a proclamation was declared against those who beheaded Charles I. At a meeting of the Maidstone council on 18 June, Broughton was officially discharged from his office and Richard Bills elected for the remainder of the term. Broughton had fled to Vevey on Lake Geneva, and was to live there until his death in 1688 at the age of 85.

OPPOSITE ABOVE: Maidstone's Wharf thrived until this century. (MM) CENTRE: The Old Mote House, the home of Sir John Tufton – a member of the Royalist Petitioners. (R)   BELOW: East Sutton House, once the home of Sir Edward Filmer.

ABOVE and CENTRE: The Friars at Aylesford, home of Mr Rycaut, one of the Royalist Petitioners. It was used by the County Committee in 1644. BELOW: Leeds Castle, home of the Royalist Sir John Culpeper, was taken over by the Parliamentarians and used to house Royalist prisoners.

ABOVE: General Lord Fairfax, leader of the Parliamentary forces. BELOW: East Farleigh Bridge over which the Parliamentarian Army passed on their way to Maidstone.

ABOVE: A view down Gabriel's Hill c1900. It is here that
some of the fiercest fighting during the Battle of Maidstone
took place. BELOW: Kits Coty House. It was from this
vantage point over-looking the Medway Valley that General
Norwich watched the Battle of Maidstone.(MM)

The Right to Rule

The present system of local government in Maidstone has developed from the Burghmote and manorial Court Leet. The people of Maidstone held a council called a burghmote which probably began in Saxon times, although the first recorded date is 1360. The Burghmote was headed by a Portreve, whose election had to be approved by the Archbishop of Canterbury, to whom the Portreve was responsible. The rest of the council was composed of 12 brethren and commoners. The Portreve acted as a magistrate and at a court called a portmote, special constables could be appointed by oath to help dispatch the burghmote's decisions.

Following the Dissolution, the end of the College of All Saints and the Fraternity of Corpus Christi, it became necessary for Maidstone to have an officially structured form of local government.

In 1549 Maidstone was granted its first charter by the young Edward VI. Dated 4 July, the document established a corporation, headed by a mayor, with 12 jurats and a commonalty. For the first time the Burghmote was freed from the heavy influence of the crown and Canterbury. It now had powers of jurisdiction over its own area, with a court where civil and criminal matters could be dealt with.

The mayor and jurats were elected by the freemen of the town, though vacancies were filled by co-option. The majority of those who held positions were landowners. A small silver-gilt mace came with the charter and to carry it a sergeant-at-mace was chosen by the mayor. The sergeant also had to announce proclamations and execute arrests on the mayor's orders. A market was granted to be held every Thursday, and a fair four times a year. The charter also signified that two burgesses could be sent to the House of Commons from Maidstone.

The Commonalty was originally synonymous with the freemen, and the first of these was not created until 1551. This status derived from birth in the town, from purchase, apprenticeships or as a gift from the mayor and jurats. Not all freemen were male. On 15 January 1645 Anne Halsnot became a freeman as she was the eldest daughter of a freeman who had no sons. Freemen had the right to vote in town and parliamentary elections, could claim a share in the profits of borough dealings, and were exempt from the town's tolls. No-one could carry on business unless he was a freeman and as late as 1762, proceedings were taken against non-freemen for trading in Maidstone. Today the title is honorary, the status having disappeared after legislation in 1835.

The rebellion of Sir Thomas Wyatt in 1554 caused the Privy Council to disenfranchise Maidstone. On 4 December 1559 Queen Elizabeth I granted the town its second charter. This expanded the grants given in 1549: the mayor was made a justice of the peace, and the inhabitants of Maidstone exempted from sitting on juries outside the town. The jurisdiction of the borough was extended, and included the river Medway between Hawkwood, near Burham, to East Farleigh. The mayor was also expected to inspect the Medway in this area, to make sure it was navigable and that the banks were in good repair. If anything amiss was spotted, such as illegal fishing, the mayor could cause the sergeant-at-mace to make arrests. This custom of the Court of Survey continues till the present day, though it no longer starts at six in the morning.

Elizabeth I's charter also clarified that the freemen of Maidstone could send two burgesses to the House of Commons. When in 1553 William Wotton and John Salwyne were elected for these posts, a dispute arose as to whether the first charter included such rights. So it was that in 1563 Nicholas Barham and Henry Fisher took their seats in parliament as the first members for Maidstone.

The Burghmote was responsible for passing by-laws such as to ensure Sunday Observance in 1562, the maintenance of hedges or fines for drunkenness. The Council also oversaw articling of apprentices to guilds. The guilds held some power in the town. In 1593 the borough was divided into wards for easier jurisdiction, with a warder for each area. By 1605 there were four companies: mercers, drapers, cordwayners and victuallers. The town was divided into four wards, each belonging to one of the companies. The warders were elected by the corporation. In 1613 the Companies were dissolved, and freemen were created by the Common Council. This was not a success and in 1621 the town was once more divided into four wards: the Town Ward under the company of mercers, Stone Ward the drapers, artisans Week Ward, and the victuallers the West Ward.

The posts of recorder and town clerk were usually a combined office until 1607, when Henry Dixon was appointed in the first single post of Town Clerk, taking over from William Gull who continued in the post of recorder which he had held since 1599. These officers were elected by the whole Council.

A third charter was granted by James I on 31 December 1604. In 1605 the first Common Council became established. To end the confusion of the Burghmote, members were elected and not co-opted. The number of the Commonalty was limited to 40, although later increased to 50. Freemen had to be members of a company before they could be admitted. With the new charter, Maidstone became a 'free town' and was granted the right to have a towngaol, and to use All Saints as the parish church.

Maidstone and several other towns were obliged to confirm the

Council's formation by acquiring a new charter. The cost of this – £160 – was raised by loans and donations. On 28 July 1619 the fourth charter was granted. With it came a visit from the heralds of the College of Arms who confirmed the town's arms. The Mayor was now able to act as coroner and the post of recorder was filled by election. The recorder and two senior jurats were made justices of the peace.

The Council was given the power to assess the inhabitants for a tax to pay the town's expenses – the first rates. They could also charge ships that docked at Maidstone a levy or toll on goods brought into the town. Any unmarked swans found on the Medway in Maidstone's jurisdiction could be claimed by the town. A fortnightly court to deal with legal issues was held in the surrounding villages.

The commonalty of 50 was felt to be too large so it was resolved that 24 to 30 men should be appointed as representatives.

The fourth charter made it clear that, where previously the mayor, jurats and commonalty could elect any freeman to serve on the council, now any inhabitant of Maidstone could be elected to serve. If they refused, they were subject to a fine.

In 1634 a dispute arose, when the vicar of All Saints, Robert Barrel, refused to make the customary announcements in church of dates of council meetings. To remedy this, the corporation bought a brass horn, which was blown before meetings at the top of the High Street, Bullock Land and Wrens Cross.

During the Civil War the corporation managed to retain its powers. When the parlimentarian Andrew Broughton was mayor, a new mace was bought. The original mace of 1549 was repaired in 1576. During the reign of James I a second mace was purchased, for the charters of 1604 and 1619 mention two sergeants-at-mace were to be appointed. In 1641 one of the jurats, Ambrose Beale, gave £30 towards a new mace but, because of the unsettled political situation, no action was taken until 1649. It was then that Broughton sold the 'little white mace' for £3 18s 4½d, and added to the earlier £30 a bequest of £10 from John Bigge, and a new mace was purchased, costing £47 3s 5d plus £1 extra for the case. The Restoration of Charles II caused the Commonwealth-style mace to be altered. A crown, costing £23 4s 4d, was fixed to its top, and the letter 'D' on this work indicates this was done in 1661.

Charles II was generally welcomed as King but his popularity waned. As he approached the end of his life in 1682, the King wished to make his brother James his heir. Parliament's support required an increase in Royal supporters in the house. As Maidstone's representation favoured the opposition, the King took action. On 20 June 1682 the Maidstone charters were sent to London and a fifth charter was granted on 26 October. Under this the way of choosing a mayor was altered. Annually, on 30 November, the feast of St Andrew, two of the jurats (now renamed aldermen) or freeholders (landowners) could be nominated for mayor by the existing mayor and aldermen. The freeholders of Maidstone would then vote for the Mayor, thus excluding the decision of the Commonalty. The 12 aldermen and 24 common councilmen were chosen by the aldermen. These changes ensured that Maidstone would support the King in the House of Commons.

In 1685 James II acceded to the throne. Unlike his brother, who tended to be a 'high' church member of the Church of England, the new King favoured Rome. To ensure that members returned to Parliament were favourable to his wishes the new King attempted to increase the numbers of Roman Catholics in Parliament. So that such changes were not too obvious, non-conformists, who were also against the Church of England, were appointed to posts. On 2 December 1687 the King sent a letter to Maidstone commanding the appointment of Joseph Wright, a baptist minister, as mayor of Maidstone. This angered many, and only the new mayor took an oath of office. On 9 January 1688 James II commanded the dismissal of seven named aldermen and 12 of the commonalty. On 22 January a further order demanded the dismissal of four more aldermen and 11 councillors. They included the Town Clerk and the Recorder. The following day new appointments were made but the recorder's dismissal was later cancelled and he was reinstated.

During 1686 and 1687 James II put Parliament in abeyance. This, along with his manoeuvres in local government, aroused much anger. He was deposed and on 5 November 1688 William of Orange brought a Protestant flavour to the monarchy. Maidstone returned to using the name of jurats rather than alderman, and matters quietened.

In the early 18th century, whichever political party held most power in the town gave the freedom of the borough to its supporters. Some freemen even lived in the poorhouse and would gladly accept bribes. Sir Robert Marsham and Thomas Bliss ensured they retained their parliamentary seats through bribery. A Whig pamphlet accused Bliss, the owner of a brewery and several public houses, of giving free beer to voters and of 'lending' money to freemen. A petition was sent to Westminster and a parliamentary committee decreed that any freeman who received alms or charity would lose the vote.

In the 1702 parliamentary election Sir Robert Marsham and Sir Thomas Roberts were elected for Maidstone. Yet another petition was produced, accusing the corporation of influencing electors by unlawful means. This resulted in the election being declared invalid, and Heaneage Finch and Thomas Bliss were elected instead.

The question then arose as to who should elect jurats. The upper bench of mayor and jurats said they alone could vote, while the common councillors on the lower bench disagreed. At a special meeting in 1715 a by-law was passed excluding the commonalty from electing jurats. This stood until 1730 when a law suit was filed on behalf of the commonalty against seven jurats who had been elected only by the upper bench. Two of the cases were argued on demurrer (a legal objection to the opponent's point) and judgement was given in favour of the common council. On this the five other jurats gave up their seats. This left the corporation with only three jurats, all of whom had been elected before the 1715 by-law.

The stalemate continued until the Burghmote Court of 10 January 1738. The remaining three jurats, one of whom was mayor, presided over the 54 freeholders present. Six common councilmen became jurats, elected by the small upper bench, and 15 inhabitants were elected to the lower bench.

Soon after, those jurats dismissed in 1730 challenged the rights of the three jurats not elected as the 1619 charter directed. One case went to court. The defending jurat lost upon which the other two jurats resigned. This left a council with just six jurats who had been elected for 1740-41.

Cases continued to be filed in 1740. The three jurats who had been replaced argued that as they had been illegally elected, the six remaining jurats they had elected were also illegal. This argument was upheld, and the remaining six jurats resigned. The Council, having no upper bench to elect jurats, was completely dissolved. The town's charter was thus forfeited. For six years Maidstone was without Mayor or Council.

In 1743 two petitions asked the Crown to grant a new charter. The Solicitor General angered both Whigs and Tories by recommending this. It was not until 1747 that, after further petitions, the Privy Council discussed a new charter. After three nights the matter was agreed and on 17 June 1747 George II signed the new charter. The document was brought to Maidstone by the local Whig leader, William Horsmonden Turner, to be met with general excitement. The charter restored the freemans' privileges, changed the date of the mayor's election to 2 May and determined that, when a vacancy occurred for a jurat, the whole Council would elect a replacement. The common councilmen would be chosen by the whole council from the main inhabitants of the town. The upper bench would also elect the recorder and the two sergeants-at-mace. The upper bench would also nominate two of the 13 jurats to be mayor. The whole council, including the 40 common councillors, finally chose the mayor by vote.

In 1758 two momentous decisions were made by the corporation. The mayor was to be paid £50 towards expenses and a new town hall was to be constructed as the Lower Court House where meetings were held was too small. It was not until 1736 that the old building was demolished and the present town hall begun. Gabriel Hanger, once a member of parliament for Maidstone, contributed £300; while the Earl of Aylesford and Lord Romney each subscribed £100. The County Magistrates provided £560 as they were to hold assizes in the new town hall. The building also contained a clock, a town bell, and a town gaol on the upper floor. The open space under the town hall was used as a market.

At the municipal election of 4 April 1764 four inhabitants opposed the council's extravagance and were elected councillors. To prevent further opposition, a majority of the council passed a by-law depriving the Commonalty of voting rights for the election of mayor, jurats, Commonalty, churchwardens and other posts such as overseers of the poor. In January 1766 the dispute came before the King's bench, and the Council's decision was overruled. So in February 1766 another by-law was passed, the right to elect common councillors being given to all council members, as well as to 40 senior freemen. The freemen appealed once more to the higher courts, but in January 1767 judgement was given against them.

On 14 March 1767 the council increased the number of common councillors from 40 to 60, making it appear that the lower bench had a majority. The freemen argued that many of the common councillors did not vote as they lived outside the town. A vacancy occured on the Council and, of the 60 freemen, only six voted and some of these lived in the workhouse. As a result, the by-law of 1764 was set aside by the King's Bench.

Voting for parliamentary members still involved bribery. Of the freemen who had a right to vote up to half lived outside the borough. In 1825, of the 795 ratepaying householders, 172 were freemen. Of the 1,578 whose rates were paid by their landlord, only 174 were freemen. Altogether only 490 of the 813 freemen lived in Maidstone.

In one parliamentary election 21 freemen hid in a hayloft until the poll for the candidates was so close, that the prospective members of parliament were willing to pay a high price for their votes.

The Parliamentary Reform Act was passed in 1832, as an attempt to improve the election system. Before 1832 the borough of Maidstone returned two members and those with votes could also elect, with other Kentish freeholders, two county members, known as knights of the shire. These county votes were cast in a small shed on the north side of Penenden Heath. In 1830 the shed was replaced by a small stone house which was eventually removed in 1877 to a position in Peel Street. All the freemen of Kent had to reach Penenden Heath to cast their county votes although it became usual after a few votes, for the polling to be concluded in Maidstone.

The Reform Act attempted to evenly redistribute parliamentary seats. Maidstone retained two, while the number of county members was increased to four. The later Act of 1885 was to allot seats by population, and was to cause Maidstone to lose one. In 1918 the boundary was enlarged from a borough to a divisional constituency.

The 1832 Reform Act still only resulted in one person in 24 having a vote. The freeman's voting qualification was altered to enfranchise all those who were 40 shilling freeholders, £10 long term leaseholders, £50 short term lease holders, or those who paid £10 a year in rent and rates. These conditions were not extended until 1918 when all men over 21 qualified, and married women over 30 qualified if their husbands had a vote. From 1928 all women over 21 received a vote, and with the act of 1945, all those who had a parliamentary vote could vote in municipal elections.

The 1832 Reform Act seemed to have little effect in Maidstone, other than the disappearance of non-resident voters. In the 1837 parliamentary election Benjamin D'Israeli stood as a prospective M P for the town. He had previously failed in High Wycombe and Taunton. D'Israeli arrived in Maidstone and called at the Bank Street home of E.P. Hall, editor of the local paper, to dictate his election address. When it came to the signature, Hall advises that the apostrophe be dropped to make the name look less foreign. From this time the young man's name became Disraeli. On 27 July 1837 he won one of the two seats at Maidstone, with 616 votes. The first member, who gained 707 votes, was Wyndam Lewis. In 1839 Disraeli was to marry the wealthy widow of Wyndam Lewis.

Disraeli became Prime Minister in 1868 and 1874, but the start of his political career was anything but smooth. In 1841 he was forced to move to another seat. It was alleged that in 1837 he had offered bribes. It was not the bribes that upset the voters but that he failed to pay them.

In 1835 Parliament passed the Municipal Corporations Act. The municipal franchise was extended to males over 21 who lived in and paid rates to Maidstone. A tenant who paid rates via his landlord did not necessarily receive a vote.

As Maidstone had a population greater than 6,000, its councillors were voted for according to ward. Councillors were elected for a term of three years and jurats six years. The term 'freeman' became an honorary title.

On 31 December 1835 the newly formed Maidstone Council held its first meeting. It consisted of six councillors from each of the High Street and King Street wards and three councillors each from Stone Street and Westborough. A further act of 1882 allowed a deputy mayor to be appointed.

The council continued to expand. In 1972 it lost its self-governing status and a new district council was formed from the areas of Maidstone Borough Council, Maidstone Rural District Council and Hollingbourn Rural District Council. The present Maidstone District Council comprises 27 wards, which return 60 councillors. The Privy Council granted Borough status and so the town retains a mayor. The first meeting was in 1974. Meetings are still held in the Council chamber of the Town Hall.

The County Council first met in April 1889 at the Sessions House of the Maidstone County gaol. In 1913 the County Hall was built, and for several years was the largest building in the town. Other buildings have been added and at Springfield a fine county library has been built.

ABOVE: Maidstone's first charter which was granted by Edward VI on 4 July 1549. (MBC) BELOW: The River Medway and All Saints Church from the present market area, during the first decade of this century. The market used to be held on Thursdays.

The Court of Survey – seen here on the River Medway at East Farleigh and attended by the Mayor– is mentioned in the 1559 Charter of Maidstone granted by Queen Elizabeth I and continues into the present day.

LEFT: These maces, c1549, remains an important part of the town's heritage and is in regular use. (MBC) ABOVE: This is how number 78 Bank Street once looked, with two storeys of decorative plasterwork which it kept until c1820. BELOW: The face of Benjamin D'Israeli can be seen on this building on the north side of Earl Street.

80

ABOVE: All Saints Church has seen many changes in style of worship since the Reformation. (MM) CENTRE: 78 Bank Street which now only retains its splendid pargetting on the first storey. It included the Prince of Wales' feathers (James I's son Henry), and the Royal Arms of Charles II. It dates from 1611. BELOW: Week Street, seen here in the early 1900s, is not much altered today except the pargetting on No 55 is no longer as clear.

ABOVE: This house which once stood in the High Street was built in 1681 by a Maidstone surgeon, Thomas Bliss, and was demolished in 1871. (R) BELOW: A detail of the pargetting on No 55 Week Street, which dates from 1680.

ABOVE: The Court Houses and Market Place in Maidstone
High Street, 1623. (R) BELOW: Lloyd George delivering a
speech to the town. (MM)

ABOVE: The Town Hall, built in 1762-3, though it was not until much later that the ground floor was enclosed. BELOW: County Hall was built 1910-13. As business in the County increased, extensions in 1936 and 1939 became necessary.

Courts and Custody

The Burghmote of Maidstone was responsible for the maintenance of law and order. Petty crime was heard at the Portmote court but more serious crimes were dealt with at the Shiremote.

The system of county assemblies had been introduced in the reign of King Edgar. In Kent the Shiremote was held twice a year on Penenden Heath. After the Norman Conquest sheriffs were appointed to run the court for the King, with the Lord Lieutenant of the County, who was usually a peer of the realm, or a powerful landowner. From 1166 Justices in Eyre held greater power than the sheriffs. At first the justices were resident in their area, but soon a system of visiting a county once every seven years was introduced. In 1215 the Magna Carta instituted annual circuits by a section of the King's bench which remained in London. With the increasing population, keepers of the peace were appointed in 1280, and in 1361 they were created justices of the peace. At the same time quarter sessions were introduced. The justices of the peace grew in number from four to five in each county, in 1361 to 30, to 40 by 1565. They had the power of Parliament behind them and in 1461 they took over from the Royalist sheriffs to hear all criminal cases, except those of treason or forgery. The sheriffs continued to hold shire courts on Penenden Heath until the late 1700s.

The quarter assizes were held at various Kentish places such as Canterbury, Rochester, and on occasion East Greenwich, Gravesend, Dartford, Sevenoaks and Maidstone. During the reigns of Henry VIII and Elizabeth I the assizes were held mostly at Rochester, but during the time of James I all except 12 assizes were held at Maidstone. In the time of Charles I and the Commonwealth 54 of the 61 assizes were held in the county town.

The assizes were held in a court house near the site of the present town hall. The building dated from the latter half of the 16th century. Here criminal cases were heard, civil hearings being held in a temporary shed constructed in the High Street or on the King's Meadow. The frame of this structure was stored between assizes in the Grammar School. In 1608 this was replaced by the Upper Court House which stood to the east of the main court house.

Prisoners were taken from the assizes to the county gaol which stood at the top of the High Street. On its castellated walls in 1590 the quarters of some traitors were displayed. The roof was flat and was used as an exercise area. The bishops gave justice in the shirecourts until 1072, when separate ecclesiastical courts were instituted. Heretics and excommunicants were held in a prison such as that of the Archbishop of Canterbury at Maidstone. Records show that it existed as early as 1255. In 1538 Archbishop Cranmer exchanged the prison and other properties with the Crown. The town or Brambles prison was used to house dissenters from the Roman Catholic faith during Queen Mary I's reign (1555). By 1648 the Brambles was being used as the town gaol, it was repaired that year and in 1659 and 1663.

A 'cage' for 'rogues and vagabonds' was attached to the Lower Court House. This was removed in 1654 to the west end of the High Street, by the bridge.

In time the County Prison became too small and some inmates had to be imprisoned in houses on the corner of Gabriel's Hill, perhaps in the deep cellars. During the plague of 1665 some prisoners were temporarily held in the George Inn, East Lane (King Street). By 1735 it was clear that a new County Prison was required and a petition was sent to Parliament. Permission was granted to build it in 1736, but little action was taken until 1744, when a site on the south side of East Lane was purchased. The assizes were held elsewhere in the county until the new prison was completed in 1746. It included two dungeons for condemned prisoners and a house for the gaoler.

Although cases of murder, witchcraft or smuggling were heard at the county assizes, the more simple cases were heard at the Burghmote or Court Leet. The county was divided into lathes. The lathe was in turn divided into further divisions called hundreds. Maidstone came into the Lathe of Aylesford. The hundred of Maidstone covered the parishes of Boxley, Barming, Detling, East Farleigh, Linton, Loose, and parts of the parishes of Bearsted, Hunton, Marden and Staplehurst. These areas were controlled by the Court Leet.

The Court Leet was the assembly of the manor and was presided over by the Lord of the Manor or his Steward. All householders who had lived in the Manor for over one year and males between 12 and 60 (70 years in early times) were called to attend the twice yearly court. In later years the court was held every other year and only attended by the tenants. Constables of the manor would be chosen and for the parishes, borsholders. Tithe collection was inspected and the services of work required by the Lord of the Manor were distributed. The repair of pavements or the problem of wandering cattle would be sorted out here and officials, such as a pound-keeper or ale-taster, were appointed. This meant the Archbishops of Canterbury had a strong hold on the affairs of Maidstone until the 1530s, when manorial rights were transferred by Archbishop Cranmer to Henry VIII. The manor of Maidstone remained a Crown possession until James I granted it in 1623 to Lady Elizabeth Finch, who became the Countess of Winchelsea. In c1630 at her death it passed to her eldest son, Thomas, fourth Earl of Winchelsea. Eventually in 1720 all the by then Astley lands in the Maidstone area were exchanged for other lands and the manorial rights were transferred to the local landowner Lord Romney of the Mote. Court Leets continued until 1835 when they ended with the Municipal Corporations Act. Lathes became District Councils in 1894.

At the Dissolution the Burghmote took over many of the Court Leet's functions. The Burghmote held a monthly court at which complaints concerning the quality of beer or bread might be brought before them. They were responsible for the upkeep of roads and bridges, and dealt with petty criminal cases where the punishment might be a fine, placing in the stocks in the High Street, or a ride on the cucking-stool.

In 1758 it was decided that a new court house should be built. The Lower Court House and the Brambles prison were pulled down in 1760, and the present town hall erected 1762-3. The County Magistrates of the western division contributed half the cost.

The court room was spacious and used for town meetings. Occasionally the room would be used for a major trial. Such a case took place in 1798 of a Roman Catholic Priest, James O'Coigley, and of Arthur O'Connor. The two men had been arrested at Margate on 1 March 1798 suspected of attempting to cross the Channel to communicate with the Revolutionary Government of France. At the time England feared the Irish wanted to ally with France against England. The Privy Council ordered that they should be tried for treason. The accused were brought from the Tower to the County Prison. The trial opened on 10 April but was adjourned until Irish witnesses could arrive and was finally opened 21 May. Several leading Whigs, who were friends of the Prince of Wales, appeared as witnesses for O'Connor. These included Sheridan, Fox, Erskine and Whitbread. Many other notable persons from high society also attended. It was after midnight on the second day of the trial when the jury retired to a house in the High Street, to return verdicts after 40 minutes of guilty on O'Coigley and not guilty on O'Connor. O'Connor attempted to leave the court room to go to a postchaise that was waiting outside the Town Hall. He was re-arrested and subsequently tried again and sent to Fort George in Scotland. In 1802 he went to Hambury and later was to become a general in the French Army. The Earl of Thanet and several others were charged with creating a riot and attempting to help O'Connor escape. Thanet was fined £1,000 and held for one year in the Tower of London.

On 7 June O'Coigley was taken to Penenden Heath for execution. To disprove rumours that he intended to commit suicide he peeled an orange at the gallows. He was then hanged but the sentence of quartering was not completed, only his head being severed and displayed to the crowd. A memorial to O'Coigley is in St Francis' Church, Week Street.

The Town Gaol was on the top floor of the Town Hall. The oak walls are covered with carved messages: 'John Davies three times here to please his wife and Scott'. Another indicates that not only his wife was pleased: 'Job wept at his misfortune, Davis smiles, 1799 three months'. Others read: 'N. Broomfield, cured and gone to Bottany Bay' and J. Pinker, gone to college to take up his degrees next March'.

This gaol proved too small. In 1798 a woman escaped across the roof into the next house. She fell 60 feet but was captured unhurt. Prisoners could call to people in the street through the windows. In 1807 a small prison was built at the back of the workhouse in Knightrider Street and some years later one was added for vagrants and petty offenders by the east end of the bridge.

Panorama of Maidstone (a copy dated 1844 from two prints by Buck, dated 1722 and 1738, showing that despite having

The 1746 County Prison was not a success. Several attempts at escape were made and the over-crowded conditions encouraged disease. Prison reformer John Howard visited it at least six times between 1774 and 1778, noted the disgusting conditions and encouraged improvements.

Due to the increase in the size of the assizes, buildings such as the Unitarian Chapel in Market Street and the Baptist Chapel in Rose Yard were pressed into service as gaols.

Eventually in 1810, 15 acres of land were bought at the north end of Week Street. The construction of the new prison was completed in 1819, and prisoners from the county and town gaols were transferred. A sessions house was added in 1826, and from 1827 the county assizes were held there.

The assizes often passed the death sentence on prisoners, although these were not necessarily carried out. In 1652 five women from Cranbrook and one from Lenham were hanged for witchcraft. Public executions were usually performed on Penenden Heath. In 1769, Susannah Lott who was convicted of poisoning her husband, was burnt to death on the Heath. During the 18th and early 19th centuries smugglers were among those executed. In December 1830 the last public execution was carried out outside the new County Prison. Some 23 men and women went to the gallows in front of the prison and further executions were held inside the prison, before public executions were abolished in 1868.

Maidstone's law keeping had remained in the power of the

a large population the town did have sufficient open space on which a temporary court building could be constructed. (MM)

constables and borsholder. From 1750 towns had the power to levy a rate for policing, and the 1833 Lighting and Watching Act permitted Maidstone to appoint a watchman. In 1836 the Maidstone Borough Police Force was formed. Four years later the Watch Committee approved the purchase of four caps and gabardines for disguises, marking one of the first attempts at plain clothes detection in England.

Kent County Constabulary was founded in 1857 and although its headquarters were at Wrens Cross, Maidstone, the Town's force remained separate. In 1921 negotiations to amalgamate the forces failed as the Borough wanted a trial period. Finally in 1943 the forces were compulsorily united by Act of Parliament. The county headquarters have been at Sutton Road since 1940, while the Maidstone station is in Palace Avenue.

ABOVE: An engraving, c1830, by J. Allen of a drawing by George Shepherd of the gaol at Maidstone. CENTRE: The Session House during the last century before the addition of the County Hall building. BELOW: The Court Leet was responsible for the repair of roads and bridges until the formation of the Borough and County Councils. (MM).

ABOVE: The County Prison at times became so overcrowded that prisoners were held in houses on the corner of Gabriel's Hill. BELOW: The County Prisons were built in 1746 on the south side of East Street – now called King Street. (R)

Carved messages on the wall of what used to be the Town
Hall Gaol. (MBC)

ABOVE:This Tudor house had its plaster front added in 1716, originally owned by the Sackville family it was once used as lodgings for visiting judges. LEFT: The Town Gaol, on the top floor of the Town Hall, can still be seen today. (MBC) RIGHT: The new surrounds the old in King Street. This attractive half-timbered estate agency is now surrounded by modern brick buildings.

LEFT: This octagonal conduit stood in the centre of Maidstone, 1567 until 1792.(MM) RIGHT: This stylish Victorian cast-iron water pump stands on the east side of Week Street, down a narrow passage.

For the Public Good

Present day Maidstone is somewhat different from the unlit, badly paved and insanitary town of the 18th century. The cost of laying paving stone in the main streets, putting up street lamps and laying down drainage was estimated in 1790 at £9,000. To meet this expense a levy of 1s 6d in the pound was made, all householders, tenants and landlords sharing the increase equally. As another means of raising money four toll gates were proposed.

The cost of these measures was not popular and farmers successfully opposed the turnpike clause in the parliamentary bill for the Maidstone improvements. During 1792-3 the plans were put into action, the conduit replaced and the main streets paved with Kentish rag and Yorkshire moor stone.

The next major improvement was the introduction of gas to the town in c1820. In 1832 a Mr Gosling sold his gas works to a group of Maidstone men who formed the Maidstone Gas Light and Coke Company. In 1858 this changed to the Maidstone Gas Company and continued to operate as such until 1949, when it became part of the South Eastern Gas Board.

Electricity was not used in Maidstone until the turn of the present century. In 1890 a provisional order to supply electricity had been obtained by the corporation which eventually decided to construct and run the company. A generating station began operation in Fairmeadow in December 1901 and subsequently main roads in the town were lit by electricity. In 1949 the company became part of the National Electricity Board.

The people of Maidstone originally used water from the springs flowing through the town. Those on Rocky Hill were used from the time of Elizabeth I, and by the 19th century water was piped across the Medway into the centre of the town. Here there were three conduits. The main one, dating from 1567, was octagonal in shape and some 24 feet in height and 8 feet in diameter. It also included a clock, lantern and bell. With the town improvements of 1792-3 this was removed, and in 1819 the number of conduits increased to seventeen. The Commissioners of Pavements also laid new iron pipes and increased the supply of water to 30,000 gallons a day in 1819. As the population of Maidstone increased so did the need for water. In 1855 it was proposed to take water out of the Medway above the Tovil stream but it was not until 1859 that two wells were sunk at Fairmeadow by the newly formed Maidstone Spring Water Company. The company constructed an Egyptian-style pumping station at East Farleigh which pumped spring water to a reservoir 300 feet higher at Barming. Thence the water flowed by gravity into the town pipes. The company grew and in 1885 bought the perpetual rights to four springs at Boarley and three at Cossington. A pumping station at Forstal helped to raise water to the higher parts of Maidstone from 1892. In 1897 a typhoid epidemic based at Farleigh necessitated the closure of pipes from Farleigh and the sinking of a well at Forstal. The Company continued, with operational difficulties, until a pumping station at Cossington and a deep well at Boxley were added in 1930. The 1973 Water Act led to the Maidstone Water Company forming part of the Southern Water Authority which has its headquarters for the Mid Kent area in Maidstone.

Today the sewage service is part of the water authority's responsibility. Maidstone had no proper sewage system until 1876, when the passing of the Rivers (Prevention of Pollution) Act meant that the town's sewage could no longer flow direct into the Medway. Work began on a sewage scheme in 1877, and by 1880 effluent was carried through pipes from the town to separating tanks at Allington. The processed sewage was then put into the Medway. This system caused the Lower Medway Navigation Company to obtain an injunction against Maidstone in 1901, resulting in the building of a proper treatment plant at Aylesford which opened in 1909.

The number of wooden-based buildings in old Maidstone led to a high fire risk. In 1591 the Burghmote Book noted the purchase of buckets, chains and hooks for use if fire broke out. In 1624 the Corporation bought two long ladders and 12 leather buckets, which were kept in the church. The modern fire service began with insurance companies, who provided assistance at fires to their premium holders. The Corporation insured the 'Court Hall' and its other properties with the Sun Fire Office in 1730. The first fire engines based at Maidstone were two hand-operated machines, which belonged to the Kent Fire Insurance Company, (1804 to 1901).

When a fire broke out in the town, water was not always available. In 1850 the supply was inadequate, and even after improvements in 1871 the water was cut off at night. The Town's water was run off four different zones of reservoir pressures and often hydrants were blocked with grit from the road, causing delays.

A volunteer fire brigade was suggested in 1855, though it was not until the Royal Society for the Protection of Life had presented the town with a fire escape in 1870, that the volunteer force was finally formed in 1873. In 1900 a Fire Brigade Committee was formed, and in March 1901 took over the Kent Fire Office's two manual pumps and superseded the volunteer brigade. Maroons were used to call firemen and telephones were not installed until 1903. A steam siren was introduced during the First World War as maroons were then illegal. The 1938 Fire Brigade Act introduced modern equipment paid for by the government and instigated the setting up of an Auxilary Fire Service (AFS). With the Second World War all fire brigades were nationalised from February 1941. In 1959 the first continental horns in Britain were tried at Maidstone and have now completely replaced the bells on firewagons. In 1967 the fire brigade left Market Buildings for the purpose-built depot on the Loose Road.

The health of the town was once blighted each year by epidemics of disease which were usually described as 'plague'. In 1562 plague prevented the Michaelmas fair and closed All Saints Church. In the following year 150 died as a result of plague. In 1580 the Council attempted to improve sanitary conditions by fining those who kept pigs in their homes. Another peak in plague fatalities was reached in 1603, when 112 died. In 1604 this dropped to 25. The August of 1625 saw attempts to prevent the plague spreading from London to Maidstone by banning trade between the two areas. In August 1636,7 men were posted to prevent people bringing plague to the town. On 18 October 1665 Sir John Banks of the Friars, Aylesford, wrote to Samuel Pepys at the Admiralty to ask that sick men should not be sent to Maidstone, as it was the only town free from plague in Kent (Pepys was to visit Maidstone in 1669).

In July 1666 several cases of plague appeared among the prisoners in the County gaol. During that hot August 70 people died; in September 106; October 110; November 24 and even in December 32 died of the plague. Only 136 died of other causes that year, plague victims totalled 347. In 1667 the plague total only reached 154.

The 18th century saw epidemics of smallpox. In 1753, 70 people died and in 1760, 100. In 1766 an Essex surgeon innoculated the poor at the workhouse where the disease was most prevelant. Even so 54 died of smallpox that year.

The 19th century brought waves of cholera and typhoid. The worst year was 1849, when there were 26 fatal cases in Maidstone. In the surrounding area, among 8,000 to 9,000 casual labourers harvesting the hops, deaths numbered 40 to 50.

The Burials Act of 1852 tackled overcrowding of the dead and 20 acres of land by the Sutton Road were bought for a town cemetery in 1858. In 1869 the death rate dropped to 26 per 1,000 but with improved sanitation this figure dropped to 14 per 1,000 by 1888. It was not until 1889 that the first sanitary inspector for the area was appointed and this led to a further decline in the death rate. Even so in 1898 there were 240 cases of diptheria, of which some 26 were fatal.

Previous to 1830 there was no hospital in Maidstone but in that year a small building was hired and two physicians and two surgeons gave their services free of charge. Running costs were met by donations which were so generous that £252 remained unspent. With this it was decided a permanent hospital should be built and in 1832 work commenced in Marsham Street. The West Kent Infirmary and Dispensary opened in 1833 to treat 1,188 people in its first year.

In 1846 a local oculist hired a building to treat eye patients. By 1851 work had commenced on the Kent County Opthalmic and Aural Hospital, to open in 1852 with a staff of three and six beds.

A Borough Isolation Hospital was opened in 1884, by which time the other hospitals had rapidly expanded.

The Care of Lunatics Act 1808 empowered the building of county asylums. The Kent asylum was not completed until 1832 when it held 168 patients and was one of the most modern hospitals of its kind. It was extended on its lands at Barming Heath in 1850, 1884 and 1906. Even more recent extensions are now being joined by the building of a new general hospital on the site.

Illness is not the only cause of distress. The care of the poor developed slowly, vagrants capable of work being severely punished, sometimes by the loss of an ear in Tudor times. Record of payments to the poor in Maidstone go back to 1585. In 1597 the Burghmote Book noted that due to lack of food many people had required poor relief and extra funds were needed. If a freeman refused to pay the newly-levied amount he would lose his status and other inhabitants would have to pay a double assessment if they refused. The 1601 Poor Law made sure that adequate funds were raised for relief. Attitudes remained harsh and in 1661 all those who received poor relief had to wear a blue and red 'P' on the sleeve of their left arm or receive no money.

In 1719 Thomas Bliss errected a workhouse in Knightrider Street, some three years before a Parliamentary Act encouraged the building of such establishments. Under the 1722 Act workhouses could be let out to contractors who used its inhabitants as cheap labour. Entry to the workhouse meant no payment of relief to an inmate. By 1770 the needs of the county had grown, and the building of a new workhouse was proposed at Maidstone. The scheme was abandoned after fierce opposition. Since 1780 Trustees of the poor overlooked the running of the workhouses. In 1834 the Poor Law Amendment Act instituted Boards of Guardians which were not abolished until 1929. From September 1835 the Coxheath Union Workhouse looked after the poor of the surrounding parishes and from 1836 those from Maidstone and from 1837 the poor from West Barming. The name was changed to the Maidstone Union Workhouse and it held 600 people, although it was later enlarged.

The Guild of Corpus Christi had maintained three almshouses in Pudding Lane and six more on the south side of the bridge. It is recorded that in 1603 those in Pudding Lane were pulled down as it was feared they might catch fire. In 1558 one Mildred Philips left a property in Stone Street to be used as almshouses and a bequest from George Langley in 1549 gave the town charge of money to be given to the poor. Other similar bequests were received by the town in 1603, 1658, 1671, 1805 and 1871.

In 1707 an armourer of London, Robert Rowland, once a native of Maidstone, left money to help apprentices to set up their own businesses but, unlike bequests of land, the money soon dwindled, and little was left by 1800.

In 1699 Sir John Banks of Aylesford left funds for the building of six almshouses. These were built on the south side of St Faith's Street and are still used as homes.

Three other almshouses were built on the north side of King Street in 1736 by Mrs Mary Duke for 'three maiden gentlewomen in reduced circumstances' who worshipped at the Presbyterian Meeting House. Edward Hunter erected the six almshouses in Mote Road in 1757. Similarly styled almshouses were built in King Street on the south side. An inscription on the building reads 'These almshouses built A.D. 1789 by John Brenchley Esq in his life time for the reception and support of decay'd housekeepers of this town and endowed with donation of £12 per anum for ever'. They are now used as offices. The almshouses in College Walk were the result of a fund raised by the one-time Mayor of Maidstone, Phillip Corrall. They were built to house the relatives of those killed in the Napoleonic Wars. In 1845 six other houses were built to the memory of Phillip Corrall in Orchard Lane.

The Cutbush Almshouses on the west side of Church Street 'were erected and endowed by Thomas Robert Cutbush' in 1865. They are different in architecture from the Cutbush Almshouses in College Avenue.

Today we are far more fortunate with help readily available, modern hospitals at hand, power at the turn of a switch, water at the turn of a tap, and facilities for leisure.

The River Medway took most of Maidstone's sewage until the construction of separating tanks at Allington in 1880.

ABOVE: In 1817 the number of conduits in Maidstone was increased to 17. This painting shows how the High Street was neatly paved up to the conduit and Butter Market. (MM) BELOW: Kent County Opthalmic and Aural Hospital which opened in 1852 with a staff of three and only six beds. OPPOSITE LEFT: This statue of Queen Victoria – a gift from Alexander Randell to the town – was erected in 1862. There is a drinking fountain at the east side. RIGHT: West Kent Hospital, originally called the Kent Infirmary and Dispensary, opened in 1833. CENTRE: The Old Mitre (left of picture), and the Kent Fire Insurance Company Building (right), drawn c1880. (R) BELOW: The Burials Act of 1852 caused the construction of the town cemetery in Sutton Road in 1858.

OPPOSITE ABOVE: Oakwood Hospital was originally Kent Asylum and opened in 1832. CENTRE: Sir John Banks' Almshouses in St Faith's Street. BELOW: The Cutbush Almshouse in College Avenue. ABOVE LEFT: The Cutbush Almshouses in Church Street, built 1865. RIGHT: These houses in College Walk were built to house the relatives of those killed in the Napoleonic Wars. CENTRE: In 1789 John Brenchley built these almshouses 'for the reception and support of decay'd housekeepers'. BELOW: In 1757 Edward Hunter erected these six almshouses in Mote Road.

ABOVE: With the suppression of the Fraternity of Corpus Christi, their Brotherhood Hall was used to house a school which was later authorised by the Town Charter of 1549. (R) LEFT: The Unitarian Church built in 1736 was the earliest Non-Conformist building in the town. RIGHT: Holy Trinity Church which contains a memorial to Captain Nolan who headed the Charge of the Light Brigade. BELOW: The Roman Catholic Church of St Francis, in Week Street.

Mind and Spirit

Until the dissolution of the Collegiate Church in 1547 Maidstone life was centred on the church. The closure of the College halted the education of the wealthier boys of the town. The date of the foundation of the first school in Maidstone is unrecorded, but one was in existence by 1348. A school may have begun with the formation of the College, and by 1450 was functioning at the College. With its closure it was decided that the school should be reopened in the Brotherhood Hall of the suppressed Fraternity of Corpus Christi. The town asked for the use of the building, and the young Edward VI's protector, Somerset, ordered that All Saint's Churchs ornaments (no longer needed since the Dissolution) should be sold to pay for it. The sale made £205 4s 0d for the Crown. The school was set up in the Fraternity Hall, authorised by the charter of 1549. It closed 1554-1558 when the town's charter was removed following the Wyatt rebellion. With the new charter of 1549 it reopened, and only scholars who could write their name and read Latin were admitted. The Maidstone Grammar School was endowed in 1574 by a wealthy cloth manufacturer, William Lambe, who in 1575 also set up the school at Sutton Valence.

Maidstone Grammar School educated several famous pupils: the poet Christopher Smart, artists James Jeffreys and William Alexander, Astronomer Royal John Pond, and Admirals Sir Robert Calder, his brother Sir Henry Calder, and Lord James Gambier. Clerics who were pupils included a Bishop of Norwich, George Horne, an Archdean of Oxford, Phineas Pett, and the chaplain to the Congress of Utrecht in 1712, William Ayhurst.

One of the most notorious ex pupils was Dr Dodd, who became tutor to the young Lord Chesterfield, and in 1776 forged a bond for £4,200 on his pupils' behalf. Despite a petition drawn-up by Dr Johnson, he was hanged at Tyburn. Staff were not without blemish. In 1691 master John Law was found guilty of murdering Thomas Wyatt – not a parent.

Following the Dissolution, All Saints became the parish church, and in 1548 its first perpetual curate, Richard Awger was appointed. In 1552 Awger also became the first Maidstone cleric to marry and consequently was deprived of his living when Mary I came to the throne in 1553. He was replaced by ardent Papist John Day. Some of the townsfolk fled to avoid persecution for their Protestant views; in 1555 two men fled to Essex, where they were captured and burnt at the stake. Others were put in the Brambles prison. William Appleby, a linen draper, and his wife left the town and hid with friends at Strood, but after two weeks were captured and imprisoned at Maidstone. On 16 June he and his wife, another couple named Edmund Allen and his wife, Joan Manning, the wife of a Maidstone victualler, Joan Bradbridge of Staplehurst and Elizabeth Lewis (known as Blind Bess) were burned at the stake in Fairmeadow. The warrant for their execution stated that their opinions were 'contrary to the determination of the dogmas of our Holy Mother, the Catholic Church, and especially concerning the sacrament of Eucharist'. The vicar of All Saints, John Day, preached a sermon at the scene, which he was to repeat in All Saints, in which he violently abused the religious dissidents. This turned the town against him, although it was not until 1563 that he was removed from this living.

With the accession of Elizabeth I there was a trend towards religious tolerance. Peter Brown, a Maidstone butcher who fled abroad in Mary's reign, returned. Suppression of Protestantism in the Netherlands in 1567 brought some 60 Dutch families to Maidstone. In 1572-3 they were joined by other fleeing Europeans. St Faith's Church was granted to the incomers for use as a Protestant chapel in 1572. The chapel had been built in the 13th century, and after the Reformation, bought by the Corporation, who in turn had sold it to Peter Maplesden, whose property passed to Nicholas Barham after the Wyatt rebellion. Barham allowed the Dutch to use the chapel, and in 1609 his son sold the land to Henry Hall. In 1624 Hall's grandson disputed the Protestants' right to use the chapel on his land without success.

The first minister of that chapel was Nicasius Van de Schure. During his ministry Reginald Scott in his *Discovery of Witchcraft* described how on 27 January 1572 ten devils were driven out of a 23-year-old Dutchman by John Sticklebow. This was supported by the mayor and other prominent townsfolk. In 1634 Archbishop Laud attempted reforms including a Dutch translation of the new English Liturgy. Laud also ruled that all first and second generation immigrants were to attend the services at All Saints. The minister of St Faith's refused and was summoned before him. As a result the chapel was closed, and several Protestant families left Maidstone.

Robert Barrel, the incumbent of All Saints during this time, was unpopular due to his high church views. When parishioners complained that Barrel demanded too much in church dues, they were fined by the Archbishop. They petitioned Parliament, claiming Barrel 'practiced and enforced antiquated and obsolete ceremonies'. In 1640 local Puritans complained that a sermon was preached only once a month. In 1643, after preaching a sermon critical of Parliament, Barrel was summoned to the House of Commons and removed from the parish.

His successor, Thomas Wilson, was a vehement Protestant. Yet

Wilson was to become unpopular too, despite his Puritan dogma during the Civil War. In 1646 he was granted the freedom of the borough, and St Faith's was reopened in 1648.

The Restoration brought a return to high church practice. An Act of Uniformity legislated against dissenters. In 1660, fifteen Quakers from Cranbrook were taken to Maidstone after a meeting, for refusing to take the oath of allegiance. They were gaoled. The same year the Anabaptists (who believed in adult baptism and common ownership of goods,) petitioned the King, explaining their refusal to take the oath and requesting release from prison. Some 20,000 Baptists in England sent a petition of Charles II, in 1661, which was presented by Thomas Grantham of Lincolnshire, and Joseph Wright of Maidstone. Though the King promised his protection, Wright was soon in Maidstone prison, where he spent a total of 20 years.

In 1662 the incumbent of All Saints, John Crump, was removed for not conforming to the Act of Uniformity, and the following year, 20 more Quakers were imprisoned.

With the Declaration of Indulgence in 1672 the Baptists were able to obtain permission to hold meetings at Tovil and Maidstone, and the Presbyterians were allowed to meet in St Faith's.

Persecution continued. Quaker Samuel Fox was fined £30 and 4 others lost goods to the value of £32 in 1681; in 1682 three people were fined £21 19s 0d simply for holding a meeting. James II sought to reduce religious persecution, to gain power for the Roman Catholics; he forced Baptist Minister Joseph Wright of Tovil and Maidstone, to be the Mayor. Only with the arrival of William and Mary, and the passing of the Act of Toleration were groups such as Baptists no longer harassed.

The earliest non-conformist building in the town was the Unitarian Church in Market Street. Built in 1736, it retains the original weather vane, and the old pulpit and gallery.

In 1747 a splinter group from the Unitarian Church formed the Independent Congregationalists and built a Church in Week Street.

The Wesleyan Methodists held services in the National School in 1774. The school used to stand on the east side of St Faith's Green. In 1805 a chapel was built in Union Street. The present chapel on the site dates back to 1823.

An independent Baptist congregation constructed a small chapel in 1807, and in 1834 built the Bethel Chapel in Union Street, which is now used by the Salvation Army.

The Baptists held meetings at Bydews in Rose Yard from 1746, but in 1823 moved to King Street. This church was rebuilt in 1862, and remained in use until the present church opposite All Saints was opened in 1906.

The 19th century also saw the building of a number of Anglican churches. Perhaps the finest was Holy Trinity in Church Street. It was designed by John Whichcord senior, twice mayor of Maidstone, and cost £13,679, of which £1,700 came from the sale of part of the recently enclosed Penenden Heath. The church was consecrated in 1828. It contains a memorial tablet to Captain Lewis Nolan of the King's Hussars, who 'fell at the head of the Light Cavalry Brigade in the charge at Balaklava on the 25 October 1856, aged 36'.

The Archdeaconry of Maidstone was separately formed from the Archdeaconry of Canterbury in 1841. From this date new churches were regularly opened: in 1841 St Stephen's at Tovil; 1857, St Philip's ; 1860, St John's (burnt down in 1960s and rebuilt on a new site); 1871, St Faith's Church, built on the site of the old 13th century chapel demolished in 1858, and in 1876, St Michael and All Angels.

The rivalry between the various denominations was most clearly illustrated in the field of education. The non-conformists supported the British and Foreign Society School which was opened in 1812 at Wheeler Street to educate 200 boys. A girls' school was opened on St Faith's Green. The National Society School was an Anglican establishment developed from a school founded in 1787, and opened in a building opposite All Saints .

Previously education was small-scale. Apart from the Grammar School, a Bluecoat School was founded in 1711 by Rev Dr Josiah Woodward, a perpetual curate of All Saints. At first the school was held in a building in the High Street, but in 1720 it moved to Knightrider Street. It continued until 1905 when its endowments were amalgamated with those of the Grammar School. In 1795 a bequest of £2,000 in government securities enabled the opening of a school in 1817 for 65 children with a master and school mistress. The money had dwindled by 1880. Sir Charles Booth opened a school in Brewer Street in 1791.

Meanwhile, the Grammar School declined, in 1818 it had only 10 day boys and 15 boarders. However, by 1849 this had risen to 20 day pupils and 10 boarders, and further increased in 1867 to 46 day boys and only 6 boarders. The school expanded quickly and in 1871 moved from the Corpus Christi Hall to a new building on the Tonbridge Road. It was further encouraged by an endowment from the Bridge Wardens of Rochester of £3,500, who also gave £6,500, to enable the opening of a Girls' Grammar School at Albion Place in January 1888.

In 1867 Rev Canon Collis founded an art college in St Faith's Street. Buildings were constructed, and in 1894 the Municipal Technical Schools of Art and Science were opened on the same site. The Technical School was later to move to the Grammar School buildings in Tonbridge Road, while now it occupies a modern block in Oakwood Park. The College of Art transferred to a new building on the same land in 1968.

The Education Act of 1870 created school boards to oversee and encourage education. By 1902 most parishes had their own school at which attendance was compulsory until 11. Secondary schools such as Westborough in 1907 and Eastborough in 1909 were founded after the council took over from the Boards. After the First World War schools increased. In 1930 the Boys' Grammar School moved to its present site, and the Girls' Grammar School moved to Buckland, off Buckland Hill. In 1944 all education passed to the County Council.

Education was not the only social issue among churchmen of the 19th century. The slave trade and its abolition was a popular subject in Maidstone, for the rector of Teston and Nettlestead, James Ramsey inspired William Wilberforce, the Member of Parliament for Hull, to make it his life's work. Ramsey had been horrified at the condition of slaves, while working as a naval surgeon. He took holy orders and went to St Kitts where he was ostracised by the white community for his compassion towards the slaves. After becoming a naval chaplain, in 1781 he came to live at Teston. Here he met friends of Miss Bouverie, who included Hannah More, John Newton and in 1783 William Wilberforce. In 1784 Ramsey published his *Essay on the treatment and conversion of African slaves in the British Sugar Colonies'* which coincided with the introduction of the Abolition of the Slave Trade Bill by Wilberforce. The slave trade was abolished in 1807, but Ramsey did not live to see this for he died in 1789.

The present Methodist Church was built in 1823, though an
earlier one stood in Union Street from 1805.

William Wilberforce continued his association with the area. Two of his sons became vicars of East Farleigh. They took a compassionate interest in the seasonal labourers, many of whom were Roman Catholic. In 1850 Rev H.W. Wilberforce was converted to Roman Catholicism. The Oxford Movement led to many such conversions. The climate was less hostile than in 1828 when between 40,000 and 50,000 people gathered on Penenden Heath to petition Parliament against the Catholic Emancipation Bill. The Roman Catholic Church of St Francis of Assisi was not built until 1880.

ABOVE: George III reviews the 22 companies of West Kent Volunteers at Mote Park in 1799, (MM) and CENTRE: pavilion erected in Mote Park by the Volunteers for the owner of Mote House, Lord Romney, Lord Lieutenant in 1801, to commemorate this visit. BELOW: The Queen's Own West Kent Regiment saw action in the Crimean War, 1854. This cannon in the High Street was captured at Sevastopol and presented to the town by Lord Panmure, Secretary of War, and George Wicks, Mayor of Maidstone.

In Time of War

Maidstone's connection with armed forces goes back to 1756 when 12,000 Hanovarian and Hessian troops were encamped on Coxheath. The commanding officers were quartered at Linton House. There was some local ill-feeling after a Hanovarian stole three silk handkerchiefs. The acting-commandant alleged that a civil court could not try a member of the foreign force. The soldier was released.

Coxheath was used as a military camp for reserve forces training to fight in the American Colonies in 1778. On 18 September manoeuvres were held on Barming Heath. On 3 November George III and Queen Charlotte reviewed the 15,000 dragoons, infantry and militia, on Coxheath. In the evening the Royal party stayed at Leeds Castle, the seat of Robert Fairfax. The following morning Mayor of Maidstone, George Bishop, presented a loyal address, after which he was knighted.

In August 1782 the 50th Foot was encamped on Coxheath. The regiment had been formed in 1741, disbanded in 1748, and reformed in 1754. It was assigned to West Kent adding this to its title, and was quartered in Maidstone in 1758 and 1780.

An army depot was set up at Maidstone in 1797, for cavalry regiments serving in India. This led to regular movements of troops through the town.

In 1794 brigades of Kent Volunteers were formed, as an extra defence force against the French. On 1 August 1799, twenty-two companies of West Kent Volunteers were reviewed by George III on Lord Romney's land at Mote Park. The King saw a force of about 5,500 from 42 settlements, the largest brigade of 267 coming from Maidstone. Eminent people present included Prime Minister William Pitt, the Secretary for State, Secretary for War, the Lord Chancellor, the First Lord of the Admiralty, and the King's military-minded second son, the Duke of York. Following this display of loyalty, a huge feast was enjoyed. Seven and a half miles of timber were required to make the tables. The food included 700 fowls, 450 dishes of beef, 400 pies, 300 hams, 300 tongues, 220 joints of veal, 60 lambs, 735 gallons of wine and 1,728 gallons of beer. Maidstone was decorated for the occasion and entertained 20,000 visitors. East Lane was changed to King Street in honour of the occasion, fireworks were set off on Fairmeadow, and on the King's orders debtors were released from prison.

In 1801 a pavilion was erected by the Volunteers in Mote Park to commemorate the review. The Volunteer companies were suspended in 1809, to be reformed in 1859, and in1908 formed part of the territorials.

During the Napoleonic war the 50th Foot, the West Kents distinguished themselves in the Egyptian campaign, earning the name 'the blind half hundred' due to the effect of the desert light. George III authorised the addition of a sphinx and the word 'Egypt' to their colours.

Fears of a French invasion grew, and on 2 August 1803 a meeting was held at Maidstone to discuss County security. The message 'We shall justify our traditional boast and prove to our Sovereign and to the World that the men of Kent will never be conquered' was sent to the King. Beacons were built on Coxheath and Blue Bell Hill, and more volunteers enrolled. On 20 August 1804 the Duke of York reviewed 10,000 troops on Coxheath, none of them Kentish.

The West Kent Regiment fought in the Peninsular Campaign and won eight battle honours, and the nickname 'the dirty half hundred' because the dye of the black uniform cuff facings was not fast.

With Napoleon's removal to Elba in 1814, the Treaty of Paris saw the closure of the camp at Coxheath. When Napoleon was imprisoned on St Helena, Richard Boys was chaplain. In 1854 Boys became the vicar of Loose, and on his death in 1866 several of his relics of Napoleon were given to Maidstone.

Following the accession of William IV, the West Kent Regiment was changed to the Queen's Own Regiment in honour of Queen Adelaide in 1831. The facings on the uniform were changed from black to blue to indicate the Royal connection. (In 1814, the 50th Foot had amalgamated with the West Kent Militia, founded 1759).

In May 1877 a review of East and West Kent Yeomanry (founded in 1794) was held in Mote Park. In 1813 various troops of yeomanry formed the East and West Kent Yeomanry Cavalry. The name of this force was changed in 1864 to Queen's Own West Kent Yeomanry.

The Queen's Own West Kent Regiment saw action during the Afghan War of 1843, and the Crimean War of 1854. A regimental depot was opened at Maidstone in August 1874. 1881 saw the amalgamation of the 97th with the 50th Foot, to form the second and first Battalions of the Queen's Own Royal West Kent Regiment, which took part in the Relief of Khartoum in 1885, and the South African War of 1900.

The West Kent Yeomanry also took part in the Boer War. Each soldier of this force had to provide his own horse, uniform and arms, and also pay his passage to South Africa. On their return in July 1901 they had an official welcome at Maidstone, and 'Imperial' was added to their title.

On 4 August 1914 the First World War broke out. The Queen's Own Royal West Kent regular battalions soon saw action, and were to serve on European and on the Near East Fronts. In Kent, volunteers formed a home defence group. They were not officially recognised until 1916, and in 1917 were issued with a uniform. The four West Kent battalions were attached to the Queen's Own.

Battalions of the Queen's Own Royal West Kent Regiment served in the various theatres of war in the Second World War. In Britain, Local Defence Volunteers were formed, later renamed the Home Guard. At Malling a Royal Air Force Station was built. In the summer of 1940 the Battle of Britain was fought over the skies of south east England. German 'planes dropped Hitler's 'last appeal to reason' on Maidstone, but the leaflets fell in the grounds of Oakwood Psychiatric Hospital, Barming. On 31 August a bomb damaged the railway at Tovil, though more serious damage was done on 2 September when two were killed and 13 injured when a bomb fell outside the West Kent Hospital in Marsham Street. On 13 September three separate incidents killed four and injured seven. The worst day was 27 September when a total of 22 were killed, 44 seriously injured and 45 slightly injured. On the last day of that month one died and 12 were injured. During October the tide turned although on 10 October a 'plane crashed on a house in Sittingbourne Road, killing nine and injuring two. That month bomb damage destroyed much property. The 9th saw one killed and one injured, and on 31 October a bomb fell at 9.00 am in Mill Street, miraculously killing only three, seriously injuring 14 and 19 others receiving minor injuries.

Sporadic air raids continued, incendiaries and V1s later caused much damage. The worst flying bomb attack was on 3 August 1944 when one exploded in the goods yard of Maidstone West railway station and killed five and injured 47. The last major incident was on 17 February when a V2 landed between the railway and London Road. The total of those who died due to action in the town was 60; seriously injured 105, and slightly injured 182.

On 30 August 1944 the Freedom of Maidstone was conferred on the Queen's Own Royal West Kent Regiment. In March 1961 the Buffs, the Royal East Kent Regiment and the Queen's Own Royal West Kents were amalgamated to form the Queen's Own Buffs, Royal West Kent Regiment. On 26 May 1962 the Honorary Freedom of Maidstone was transferred to the renamed regiment.

Leeds Castle, the seat of Robert Fairfax. George III stayed
here after reviewing 15,000 troops on Coxheath. (KCL)

LEFT: Napoleon's chair, given to the town by one time
chaplain of St Helena, Richard Boys. (MM) RIGHT: The
War Memorial in Brenchley Gardens. BELOW: The
Queen's Own Regiment, c1850.

114

ABOVE: The West Kent Yeomanry attending the
proclamation of Edward VII in 1901. (MM) BELOW:
When a bomb fell in Mill Street on 31 October 1940 three
were killed and 33 injured. The town's transport was badly
disrupted because the trolley wires were detroyed.

115

ABOVE LEFT: William Shipley's home in Knightrider Street. RIGHT: His tomb in All Saints Churchyard. CENTRE: The new Mote House designed in 1793 by Daniel Asher Alexander, who later designed Maidstone and Dartmoor prisons. LEFT: The Corn Exchange, originally designed by Whichcord and Ashpitel, has recently regained much of its charm having been re-paved. RIGHT: 8-9 High Street. This fine building with its Ionic columns was designed by Whichcord senior.

Town of Talents

Today the Master's House of the old College is the Kent Music School, and Maidstone has a large number of music societies. The earliest of the town's famous musicians was John Jenkins (1592-1678). Son of a Maidstone carpenter who lived in East Lane, he followed his father's interest in music. His talent led to patronage by powerful Norfolk families, and he even played the lyra viol for Charles I. After the Restoration Jenkins was appointed as a theorbo (a large lute) player at Court. He spent little time at court, and was to die at Kimberly, Norfolk in 1678. He left over 1,000 compositions – a pioneer in music for stringed instruments, especially viols.

In 1836 the Maidstone Amateur Harmonic Society was founded. Famous musical figures of the period played for the society, including Fanny Burnett, sister of Charles Dickens, and her husband Henry Burnett. They met while studying singing at the Royal Academy of Music. In 1838 Robert Lindley shared a music stand with the World famous double bass player Dragonetti. An instrument that had belonged to Dragonetti was one of those in the collection of Charles Gustavus Whittaker of Barming Place. Part of the collection is now in Maidstone Museum. The Novello family was also connected with the musical life of the town.

Theatres were originally temporary structures, such as the 'New Theatre' which was built near the river for two weeks in December 1778. The first recorded theatre was begun c1803, and was run by Mrs Sarah Baker. It was 85 feet by 23 feet in size, had three entrances, and over the main one hung a picture of Shakespeare by the local artist, William Jeffreys. A young unknown called Edmund Kean appeared there. The building was demolished in 1851.

The fine Queen Anne house in Knightrider Street was the home of William Shipley (1714-1803), who in 1750 founded the St Martin's Lane Academy, where several famous artists worked. With the help of Lord Romney of the Mote, Maidstone, Shipley also founded the Society of Arts for 'the encouragement of arts, manufacture and commerce in Great Britain' in 1754. In 1769 he moved to Maidstone and, with Romney, formed the 'Society for the Promotion of useful knowledge'. This society worked on projects such as the improvement of prison conditions, following an inquiry in 1783. Shipley died at Maidstone in 1803 and is buried in All Saints churchyard. The society he founded became the Royal Society of Arts in 1908.

117

The townscape reflects several famous architects. In 1794 Daniel Asher Alexander (1768-1846) designed the new Mote House, and in 1811 the Maidstone County Prison. On the latter he was helped by a Scots-born architect John Whichcord. Whichcord joined forces with William Ashpitel, and the partnership designed several important Maidstone buildings. Their sons, John Whichcord junior (1823-50) and Arthur Ashpitel (1807-69) continued the practice. Buildings designed by the group include Holy Trinity Church, 8-9 High Street (1827), The Corn Exchange (1835), The Opthalmic Hospital (1846), and 93-95 High Street, which is an early example of an iron-framed building, dated 1855.

Local artists include William Woollett (1735-85) who was born in Rose Yard. His father won a share in a lottery prize, and bought The Turk's Head in King Street. Here young William was noticed for his engravings on pewter beer pots. He was apprenticed to John Tinny, and in 1761 was commissioned to engrave a picture by artist Richard Wilson. In 1775 he was appointed Engraver in Ordinary to George III.

James Jeffreys (1751-84) was a pupil of Woollett, and the son of local painter William Jeffreys. After his apprenticeship to Woollett, James entered the Royal Academy School in 1772. Two years later he won the gold palette of the Society of Arts, for historical drawing, and in 1775-8 was a Rome Scholar, becoming one of the prominent English artists in Rome.

William Alexander (1767-1816) was born at Boxley. In 1792 he went to China as the official draughtsman to the First British Embassy there, and produced many fine water colours depicting his travels. Arthur Hughes (1832-1915) was a Pre-Raphaelite, who lived in Maidstone at the same time as John Brett (1830-1902) who was also under the influence of the Pre-Raphaelites.

Perhaps the most impressive local artist was Albert Goodwin (1845-1932) who painted atmospheric landscapes in England and Europe. His brothers Harry and Frank were also artists in their own right. Example of the Goodwins' works may be found in the excellent collection at Maidstone Musuem Art Gallery.

Maidstone has attracted writers as well as artists and musicians. Poet Christopher Smart (1722-1771) came to Barming when his father became rector of the local church in 1726. On his father's death in 1732 Christopher was sent to Maidstone Grammar School until 1739, when he entered Pembroke Hall, Cambridge. Here he was made a fellow until his marriage, when he was contracted to a book-seller for 99 years to write tales. Depressed by family problems, he was sent to Bedlam, and after his release, arrested for breaking the publisher's contract. He ended his life in prison. Today he is remembered for his pastoral poetry, especially his descriptions of hop fields.

William Hazlitt (1778-1830) was born in Rose Yard. His father was the minister of the Unitarian Church in the parallel Market Street.

William accompanied his father to America in 1783 but returned in 1786 to study for the church. When he met a Unitarian preacher called Coleridge he was introduced to the famous lakeland writers of the time. Hazlitt took an interest in painting, but found fame as an essayist, and as the founder of modern dramatic criticism.

Charles Dickens featured Maidstone in his work. The Manor Farm, Dingley Dell in *Pickwick Papers* has been identified as Cobtree Hall, whose owner William Spong has been suggested as the prototype for Mr Wardle. The town of Muggleton in *Pickwick Papers* is almost certainly Maidstone, though the cricket match may have taken place at West Malling.

The poet Tennyson often stayed with his sister and her husband, Edmund Law Lushington, at Park House, Boxley, (demolished 1955). The area inspired settings for poems such as *Queen Mary* in which he used Allington Castle, or *The Brook* which rose in the vicarage garden at Boxley and flowed through the estate of Park House, entering the Medway opposite the castle at Allington. The later poet, Edmund Blunden (1897-1974) spent much of his youth at Yalding where his father was master of the village school.

Journalism has a long history in Maidstone. In 1725 *The Maidstone Mercury* was published for a short time by J. Watson of the High Street 'near the conduit'. The first regular newspaper was *The Maidstone and Kentish Journal* established in 1786, and continued until 1912. In 1812 *The Maidstone Gazette for Kent Sussex Surrey and Essex* began publication, though in 1852 it adopted the name *South Eastern Gazette*. *The Maidstone Telegraph* was founded in 1860, and quickly grew to overtake its rivals. From this grew the present *Kent Messenger*.

Not everyone could afford to read newspapers or books, so reading clubs emerged during the 19th century. The first town library arose from the bequest of books and antiques by Dr Thomas Charles, owner of Chillington Manor. In November 1855 a reference room was opened at the Manor. The first lending library opened with donated books in 1890, and in June 1899 the Victoria Library was officially opened by the Lord Mayor of London. In 1948 a qualified librarian was appointed. In 1964 the library moved to the present modern building, and is now part of the County Library service.

The Charles bequest to the Borough of 1855 formed the backbone of the Maidstone Museum collection. The council bought Chillington Manor in 1857 and it was opened as a museum the following year. In 1867 Julius Brenchley, a Victorian explorer of the Americas, Australasia and the Far East gave his fine ethnological collection to the town, and £400 towards an extension. In 1873 he presented Maidstone with the land that now forms Brenchley Gardens. The museum gradually expanded; in 1874 the 15th century south wing of Court Lodge, East Farleigh was rebuilt next to the museum, and in 1890 the Bentlif Art Gallery was added, to house the Bentlif Collection of pictures. There were further extensions in 1897, 1923 and a rebuilding programme during this decade.

For those who enjoy less studious forms of relaxation Maidstone has several societies covering the main sports. There is a Sports Centre at Oakwood Park, and the grounds of Mote Park include swimming baths that in 1976 replaced the Victorian baths that stood in Fairmeadow since 1851.

Golf may be played on courses at Bearsted, Leeds and West Malling. Maidstone Rugby Football Club is one of the oldest clubs in the country, and existed before its records began in 1880. Maidstone United Football Club was formed in about 1897 from the older Invicta Club. It had several successful seasons, and became professional after World War One. It returned to amateur status until the 1970s when it once more turned professional, and now plays in the Southern League, Premier Division.

Maidstone and District Bowls League was founded in 1925, but the Burghmote Book of 1666 mentions that a bowling green had been recently laid out above Fairmeadow. Older sports include bear baiting and a book published in 1672, Swinock's *Life and Death of Mr Thos Wilson, minister of Maidstone* includes a list of sports played in the 'very profane town . . . on the Lord's day' including Morris dancing, cudgel playing, stoolball and cricket.

The Mote Cricket Club was founded in 1857, and the first County Cricket Club was founded at Maidstone in 1859. Many famous cricketers have played at Mote Park including Frank Wooley and Colin Cowdrey. The ground at West Malling is also historic and the village green at Bearsted is said to be one of the oldest cricket pitches in England. Alfred Mynn, who was the first eminent bowler to use over arm bowling, played there.

Cricket was certainly played at Maidstone as far back as 1646, when a court case concerning an unpaid wager on a game of cricket is recorded in the Burghmote Book. This game was played between two teams of local gentry on Coxheath 'in the parish of Boughton Monchelsea'. One of the first recorded games took place at Malling in 1705 between West Kent and Chatham teams. The Kent team played at Coxheath in 1736, though the first county match was not until 1777. In 1807 a cricket match was played on Penenden Heath between 13 All England and 23 men of Kent for a wager of 1,000 guineas. Kent won by 162. The correct sporting wear was a light shirt, thin white cord breeches, almost transparent stockings, silk socks and a top hat with a flattened crown. Batsmen were often declared out by their hats falling onto the wicket.

ABOVE: 93-95 High Street, an early example of an iron-framed building of 1855. Designed by Whichcord and Aspitel. LEFT: William Hazlitt was born in Rose Yard. (MC) RIGHT: James Jeffereys, son of a local painter, became one of the prominent English artists in Rome in the late 18th century. (MM) BELOW: Maidstone Museum

ABOVE: Maidstone High Street as painted by G. S. Shepherd in 1829 – showing that the centre of the town has been a busy shopping centre for many years. (MM) BELOW: Maidstone Bridge in c1860 showing a thriving wharf.

122

Markets Fair

As the settlement developed, the town became the centre of trade for the surrounding area. In 1261 Archbishop Boniface obtained permission from Henry III to hold a market each Thursday on Petersfield near the hospice of St Peter and St Paul. A Tuesday market and a three day fair on the feast of the Cross held at the Mote, were granted by the King in 1267.

A grant of standard weights and measures to be held at Maidstone, indicated that by 1496 the town had considerable commercial importance, though real expansion did not take place until after the Dissolution, with the grant of the town's first charter. This allowed a town market to be held on Thursdays in the High Street. A note in the Burghmote Book of 1564 records that the market ran from nine in the morning to three in the afternoon, a bell marking commencement and closure.

It was run on strict rules; tolls were charged on cloth or cattle brought into Maidstone for sale. The people from country areas were only allowed to sell produce on market days; selling on other days would attract a fine. In 1600 it was noted that outside market times only food and drink (but not meat) could be sold to 'foreigners'. Weights were provided for use by butchers, who were charged 1d for the privilege in 1589. The market gradually extended its hours, and in 1629 trading was forced to end at six o'clock in the summer, and four o'clock in winter-time.

Four annual fairs were held by 1570, when records show that the May, Mid Summer and St Faith's fairs were held on Queen's Meadow while the Candlemas Fair was held in the High Street. By the time of James I the fairs were held on 2 February (Candlemas Fair), 1 May, 9 June (the Garlick or Midsummer fair) and the Michaelmas or Runt Fair on 6 October. These dates had altered by the 18th century to 13 February, 12 May, 20 June and 17 October respectively The latter fair was the largest, consisting of a stockmarket held in Bullock Lane.

A cornmarket was held under the market cross in the High Street until 1608, when it was transferred to under the upper Court House, the corn being stored in a room above the court. At this time a monthly fish market was held under the market cross.

In 1751 George II granted a cattle market to be held every second Tuesday of each month. Previously a small stock market had been held in Bullock Lane; the new market was held in Lock Meadow. A hop market was granted in 1766, showing the increased importance of Maidstone as an agricultural centre.

A shambles where butchers traded was sited to the west end of Middle Row and lower down the High Street was a Butter Market, where dairy products were sold. In 1806 an octagonal structure was built over the Butter Market.

The Market increased in size, and in 1771 the market cross was moved into the site of the old gaol. In 1780 the cross was demolished and a purpose built structure for a fruit and vegetable market constructed. This was demolished in 1805 and a new market built incorporating a corn market. By 1823 the congestion of traffic in the High Street was so bad that a committee was appointed to look at the market. The existing buildings were found to be unsatisfactory or in need of repair. Work began on a site off the High Street in March 1825. The new buildings were opened a year later. Even this did not prove satisfactory, and in 1835 the present Corn Exchange was built, with stalls underneath. Later some of the stalls in Earl Street were turned into committee rooms, and in 1869 a concert hall was added. In 1900 the stalls at the High Street end were converted into a fire station, and others became covered shops.

The weekly stock market moved in 1825 from Bullocks Lane to the Town or Fair Meadow, though it was not until 1892 that the town purchased Lock Meadow, on which to hold the agricultural fairs during May, June and October. In 1914 an agricultural hall was built on the site. In 1920 the whole market moved from Fair Meadow to Lock Meadow, where it continues to be held.

One factor behind Maidstone's growth as a market town was its accessibility. The higher ground running east-west provided firm land on which roads could be made, and the Roman Road was the basis of the north-south route. The river Medway provided a water route, but it was tidal up to East Farleigh, and too shallow west of there. At low tide the river could be forded between All Saints Church and Lock Meadow, and St Peter's Church and Corpus Christi Hall.

Though water transport was slower and less direct than overland, it provided a cheaper means for carrying heavy goods such as quarry stone, Wealden iron or timber. Water transport offered a smoother journey, protecting fragile goods, such as locally grown fruit.

Maidstone had several wharves, mainly sited by Fair Meadow. There were four in 1570, and the town had four hoys – sea going vessels ranging from 22 to 50 tons. The trade was considerable and from 1619 the Town Charter authorised tolls on vessels and cargoes stopping at Maidstone.

To improve the Medway navigation an Act was passed in 1628. A later Act of 1644, inspired by the work of Dutch engineers in the Low Countries, facilitated deepening of the Medway, the construction of a tow path, and locks to control the water. It was not until 1739 that an Act of George II made the Medway navigable above Maidstone, allowing barges of 40 tons to reach Tonbridge via locks. This further increased the through trade, and Maidstone's usefulness as a market centre. During the 1774 hop-picking season, barges left Maidstone three times a week for London.

In 1792 the Lower Medway Navigation Company, formed in 1740, built the important tidal lock at Allington, where previously there had only been a ford. By 1809, 25 barges were trading from Maidstone. This had doubled by 1834, encouraged by the completion of a canal from Strood to Gravesend in 1824, which cut the distance between Maidstone and London from 70 to 40 miles. Railway development was to take much of this freight traffic and eventually the Thames Medway canal was filled in and used from 1846 as part of a railway route. River trade gradually declined, although 19th century industries were sited on the riverside.

Before 18th century improvements in road travel, road conditions varied. Since 1555, each parish had been responsible for the roads within its boundaries, each man giving four days' work a year towards maintenance. This was not abolished until 1835. With the introduction of wheeled carriages in the 17th century, Parliament had to legislate to restrict the size and weight of vehicles. From 1663 turnpike roads were introduced. Usually a trust was formed by landowners to construct and maintain roads by charging a toll. The Rochester to Maidstone road was the first road to be turnpiked locally – in 1728. Most other roads were built 1750-1780. A turnpike gate stood at the west end of the bridge until 1772 when it was moved up the London Road. The Turnpike Trusts on the London and Tonbridge Roads did not end until 1870 when responsibility passed to the local authority, and until 1888, when the County Council was formed. From about 1550 the Corporation of Maidstone employed messengers, but a postal service was not set up until 1641. Henceforth a post left for London on Monday, Wednesday and Friday, and those who carried letters without the Mayor's sanction were subject to a ten shilling fine. Maidstone was not included on the official table of post towns until 1669, and the service quickly grew to a daily post (except Sundays) by 1672. The post was collected at Rochester. In 1675 the route was extended to Lenham, to Malling in 1676, and in 1677 the Dover Post Route included an official branch to Ashford via Rochester and Maidstone. The Maidstone to Tonbridge route was not opened until 1802. A direct route from London to Maidstone was introduced in 1836. Till 1772 the postmaster, or a person he employed delivered the letters, collecting payment from the recipients. From 1772 the Post Office was responsible for free house-to-house delivery, and in 1840 pre-paid letters and adhesive stamps were generally introduced.

The post travelled by horse or donkey cart until about 1806 when coach travel reached Maidstone. In 1836 eight coaches travelled from London to Maidstone 82 journeys a week.This was only exceeded by Dover and Canterbury which had 94 and 92 postal coaches a week respectively. Mail coaches carried passengers, and stage coaches rivalled them for business. By 1839, stage coaches ran daily from Maidstone to Ashford, Canterbury, Dover, Hastings or Tunbridge Wells.

Mail and stage coaches were dramatically superseded by the train. The South Eastern Railway had planned to take its main line from London to Dover via Maidstone but landowners opposed,this so when the line opened in 1842, the nearest station (Maidstone Road, now Paddock Wood) was ten miles from the county town. A branch line to Maidstone was sanctioned in 1843, and one year later, on 25 September 1844, the first train ran along the single track to the town. The engine was called *Kentish Man* and all the passengers were carried free of charge.

Maidstone tradesmen feared the trains would take much of their business to London, but the reverse happened. Soon the line was a double track and equipped with an electric telegraph, of which the South Eastern Railway was a pioneer. In 1853 an extension to Strood was sanctioned, the line opening 18 June 1856 with a new Maidstone West Station building.

An alternative line was planned in 1862 by the Sevenoaks,,Maidstone and Tonbridge Railway, who were later to become part of the London, Chatham and Dover Railway. Maidstone East Station did not come into operation until 1 June 1874 when the London, Chatham and Dover Railway Company extended their line from Oxford. This also met opposition, for farmers feared the 'London Smash'em and Turnover' trains would frighten stock. It transpired that track could be laid over land at Barming on condition that one train a day stopped, thus bringing about the construction of Barming Station, two miles from the village. This line was double tracked in 1881, and three years later extended to Ashford.

As late as 1905 a proposal was made by the Kent and East Sussex Railway to build a branch line from Headcorn via Sutton Valence and Loose to Maidstone. Gradients and lack of money prevented its construction, although the plans did receive government approval.

Local public transport in the 19th century consisted mainly of horse drawn 'buses, and these were gradually replaced by trains after the introduction in 1904 of a tramcar route from the depot at Barming to Maidstone. This service was extended to Loose in 1907. Motor omnibuses in turn replaced trams in 1920. The first motor route from London Road to Penenden Heath began in 1924. The last tram ran in 1930, the tram routes converted to trolley buses from 1928. The motor 'bus routes were increased, and the last trolley 'bus ran in 1967. In 1967 the 'bus depot moved to Armstrong Road, and the service continued to be run by Maidstone Borough Council.

Longer routes had been suggested as early as 1902 when a tramway was proposed to link Chatham and Maidstone. This route was not covered by public transport until the introduction of four chain driven 'buses in 1908 by the Maidstone and District Company, founded by Walter Flexman French, proprietor of a 'cycle shop, carried on by his son, the late George Flexman French, who continued to manage it after its amalgamation into the BET Group. A single fare to Chatham was 8d, or 2d extra to sit beside the driver. At night the 'bus chassis was removed so that goods could be transported to London. The company quickly grew and in 1921 opened its Gillingham depot. In 1922 it moved from St Peter's Street to Palace Avenue, where it has continued to operate as part of the National Bus Company.

ABOVE: Transport at Aylesford by horse, cart and boat.
BELOW: Maidstone High Street has seen many changes,
but a number of buildings have survived.

127

ABOVE: Maidstone East Station still reveals some of its original architecture. CENTRE: By daytime this vehicle was used for public transport, by night as a lorry for carrying goods such as hops. (MM) BELOW: The staff of the Maidstone tramway with the Mayor. (MBC)

LEFT: The opening of the Maidstone tramway, 14 July
1904. RIGHT: How the townsfolk once travelled. BELOW:
The last horse-drawn 'bus in Maidstone.

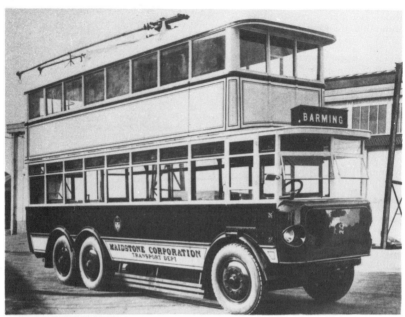

Maidstone's public transport. (MBC)

Wealth Through Industry

Maidstone prospered not simply through position, but because its well-drained soil was suited to many crops; the rivers Medway, Len and Loose, provided water, and power for water wheels in the Len and Loose valleys, while wood and stone for building materials were abundant.

Rivers also provided food. The Domesday Book mentions that Maidstone had two eel fisheries, and fish have been caught in small quantities from earliest times. By the 18th century a flourishing fish market had developed, with the Medway as a link with the north Kent coast.

The extensive woodlands around Maidstone were used early on for fuel, as building material for traditional Kentish weatherboarding and as a basis for timber-framed buildings. A forestry industry developed and large oaks, such as those in King's Wood to the south east of Maidstone were sent to the naval dock yards at Chatham for ship building. Oak bark was used by local tanners. The quick growing Spanish or sweet chestnut with its long straight trunk was in demand for hop poles from the 17th century, and today is still grown for this purpose and for palings.

Local rag stone quarries provided material for the Roman wall of the City of London, for part of the Tower of London, for Hampton Court, Westminster Palace, Eton College, Rochester Cathedral, Castle and Bridge as well as in local buildings. In 1348, ragstone from Maidstone and Aylesford was sent by river to Cheapside 'for Queen Philippa's great wardrobe' and in 1541 was used to rebuild the walls of Calais. Ragstone was also used for cannon balls. In 1418 Henry V endorsed an order for 7,000 cannon balls and in 1534 some 1,214 cannon balls were sent to the Tower of London.

Fine sand from the Folkstone Beds at Bearsted, Thurnham, Hollingbourne and Aylesford were used for writing sand (for 'blotting' ink) and later in glass production, notably the lead glassware of George Ravenscroft, during the 17th century.

Gravel pits in the Medway valley increased during the last century, and continue to supply the building industry. Local clay has been used in brick-making, but the invention of Portland cement by Joseph Aspdin in 1824 led to the development of a modern cement industry. Made by burning chalk from the Downs and river clay, which after heating is ground into a powder, it has become a major ingredient of modern building construction. The population of villages in the Medway valley to the north of Maidstone doubled or trebled in size during the 19th century due to the rapid expansion of the cement industry.

Another type of clay called fullers earth was used to remove the natural oil from locally-woven woollen cloth. This clay was so valuable to the cloth industry that in 1640 its export was prohibited. In 1641, one hundred and twenty cauldrons, (one hundred cauldrons being 36 bushels) were sent to Hull for use in the Yorkshire cloth industry. The presence of local fulling pits encouraged the growth of cloth weaving in Maidstone.

Sheep on the North Downs and in the surrounding area provided wool which, when woven, produced a rather coarse-textured fabric. Even so, Kentish wool was valued by European weavers. To encourage the development of an English cloth industry, and to prevent any further economic gain by European weavers, Edward III in 1331 invited John Kemp of Ghent and his workers to settle in England. The foreign weavers settled at Cranbrook, where their skills were soon passed on to the indigenous population. Six years later, when Parliament was held at Rochester, an act was passed to encourage Flemish weavers to settle in England.

Several foreign weaving families came to live in Maidstone. By 1552 Drapers' and Mercers' companies had emerged. In 1567 some 60 Protestant families, refugees from the Roman Catholic rule of the Duke of Alva, came to Maidstone. They were joined in 1573 by more refugees. The weavers hired houses and employed local people. The 'dochemen' are occasionally mentioned in the town's account books, and by 1585 they numbered 120 adults. In this year it was felt that as they were no longer aliens, duty on their products of fustian, grogram (silk and mohair), a linen and wool mixture called linsey, woolsey and patterned cloths, should be reduced.

Woollen cloth was produced after several processes, including washing, using water and fullers earth. Originally this was done by treading or walking in troughs, but the introduction of fulling mills reduced labour. Water wheels were built over the fast running rivers of Len and Loose, and in turn drove hammers which beat the cloth. Nearly all the watermills on the Len were put to this purpose until about 1700 when the Yorkshire cloth industry removed much of the trade, the last fulling mill in the Maidstone area closing in about 1820.

After fulling, the cloth was dried, brushed and loose ends of thread trimmed. The product was then checked for quality. In 1569 two warders of Maidstone did this job, one a local man, the other one of the foreigners. A law of 1552 stated that a Kentish broadcloth was 28 to 30, later 34, yards in length, 58 inches wide and when wet weighed 90 lbs – 66lbs when dry.

The Dutch not only brought weaving skills with them. Although flax was already grown in England, the refugees may well have introduced it to Kent as a cash crop. The flax fibre was spun and woven into cloth, and this linen was used for cloths and sheets, but also supplied a demand for canvas sails and ships ropes for the Chatham naval yard. Linen thread making, known as 'Dutch work', was recorded locally in 1571. By the 17th century Maidstone was the centre for linen thread production, an industry that continued until the mid 18th century.

The Civil War depressed the Maidstone cloth trade. Many employers could no longer afford to pay their workers, and cheap imported cloth further decreased the demand. An influx of French Huguenots in 1685 introduced other textile skills, but the trade failed to recover. The invention of machine spinning and weaving, and their introduction in the north of England finally killed the southern industry. Small amounts of flax were grown to produce linen hop bags, but the introduction of cheap jute from 1859 ended even this production.

Local farmers often depended upon flax to provide them with a cash profit, most of their produce being little more than self-sufficient. The decline of the linen trade led to alternative crops, notably soft fruits and hops. Animal husbandry included sheep, pigs, a few dairy cattle and substantial beef stock production sold at the Maidstone fairs. In 1724 Daniel Defoe commented 'From the wild of Kent, which begins about six miles off . . . (from Maidstone) . . .they bring large Kentish bullocks, fam'd for being generally all red . . . they are counted the largest breed in England'.

Defoe described the cherry orchards as being 'the largest in England' and fruit growing has proved an important part of the local economy. Fruit was not only sold in the local market but in London. In 1899 George Bunyard, a local horticulturalist began to pack fruit in non-returnable containers and to grade his produce. The East Malling Research Station has become famous for research into plant diseases and the development of new plant breeds.

Locally cultivated hazel trees have long been famous for their Kentish cobnuts. In the 17th century much of the locally grown wheat was sent to London, while barley was used in the Maidstone brewing industry.

Tradition says that 'Turkeys, Carp, Hops, Pickeral and Beer; Came to England all in a Year' the year being 1424. Certainly in 1426 information was laid against a Maidstone person for putting 'an unwholesome weed called the hopp in beer'. Henry VIII disliked the flavour, and the herbalists, fearing they were to lose trade, persuaded the King to legislate against the use of hops in beer. Yet by 1549 the hop's popularity had proved so great, that the Privy Council issued a warrant for £140 'for charges in bringing over certain hop setters' in order to help the English farmers learn how to cultivate it, and to reduce the amount of imported hops.

Farmers quickly realised that although the hop was expensive to cultivate, it gave them a good return on their investment. The government were quick to realise the hop would make a taxable commodity and introduced a duty on hops, paid by the grower according to his acreage. By 1636 Maidstone had weights for hops, and the Town Charter of 1682 gave permission for a hop fair to be held.

It was during the 18th century that hop cultivation became paramount. Soon itinerant labour was required for each hopping season. Every year large numbers flooded into Kent the tradition only ending with the mechanisation of the late 1930s. Maidstone was the centre of the Kentish hopping industry.

Maidstone, with hops, barley and sources of water readily available, developed a brewing industry. The first record of a Maidstone brewery is in 1650 when a Lower Brewery in Stone Street was owned by John Saunders. The name suggests that an Upper Brewery existed, although such a named brewery in Brewer Street is not mentioned for several years. By 1700 both these establishments were owned by the Brenchley family, but ownership changed so that they were once more separate establishments until about 1820 when the Upper Brewery was bought by the Lower Brewery, the building demolished and the land sold. The Lower Brewery finally closed when the owners, Isherwood, Foster and Stacey amalgamated with Fremlin Brothers and the land was sold in 1930.

The Medway Brewery was built in 1799 by William Baldwin on land leased from the Earl of Romney. The company flourished and passed to Baldwin's son, on whose death in 1866 the brewery became Holmes and Style. Holmes died in 1882, and the company amalgamated with Chatham brewers to become, in 1899, Style and Winch. This was in turn later amalagamated with Courage and Barclay.

In 1861 Ralph Fremlin of Wateringbury founded his company in an almost derelict brewery in Earl Street. Fremlin sold his beer by delivering to customers' homes as well as public houses, and his business soon expanded, his three brothers joining the enterprise. The company absorbed other companies and the family crest of an elephant dates from the Fremlin family's connection with the East India Company. The company is now part of the Whitbread Fremlins group.

Cider was made from local apples by 1800 when Mr Stone owned a large press. Gazle wine, made from blackcurrants, was also a popular local beverage. In 1785 George Bishop established a gin distillery. After facing government opposition, he gained permission by arguing that home production would reduce both legal and illegal imports. His gin quickly gained fame, although after Bishop's death the company went into decline and closed in 1818.

In 1774 Thomas Grant founded a distillery at Dover, but after a cliff fall in 1853 the company moved to Maidstone – Grants Morella Cherry Brandy, produced from locally grown fruit. The secret of the constituents of the drink were handed down through the Grant family until the death of the founder's great great grandson in 1960.

Maidstone's paper industry mainly dates back to 1680, although there may have been paper makers among the refugees of 1567. John Speilmann set up a paper mill some twenty years later, at Dartford, probably using skilled refugee labour. After the Civil War the paper industry rapidly expanded. There was not enough parchment available, and the development of printing had increased demand for paper. The 1680s saw the collapse of the linen trade, and also an influx of Huguenots, several of whom may have been skilled in the paper trade. During this decade, fulling mills, most notably those of the Loose valley were converted to paper production.

One of the most famous, Turkey Mill, was first mentioned in 1629 when it was a fulling mill converted by George Gill during the 1680s. By 1719 the mill was run by his son, producing white and brown papers. William Gill went bankrupt in 1731; the mill was purchased by Richard Harris. Harris died, and in 1740 his widow married James Whatman, who ran the firm until his death in 1759. It was managed by Anne and their son until 1794 when the young James Whatman sold his Turkey, Poll and Loose Mills. Turkey Mill then became the property of two brothers, Finch and Thomas Robert Hollingworth, with another partner, William Balston. This partnership was dissolved in 1805, but the company continued in the ownership of members of the Hollingworth family and their descendants, finally closing in 1976.

William Balston began his own business at Springfield Mill in 1806 and in 1807 installed a Boulton and Watt steam driven beam engine of 36 horse power and a boiler of 42 horse power, which continued in use until about 1900. In 1808 the Fourdrinier brothers wrote to Balston suggesting that he installed one of their paper making machines. Balston rejected the idea, leaving others to be more adventurous. The mill ran into financial difficulties, but was saved by Godfrey Bosanquet and William Gaussen. It prospered until a mill fire in 1863. Since the First World War the company has specialised in filter papers and is now part of the Whatman Company.

Lower Tovil Mill dates back to 1650 although it did not become a paper mill until later. It changed hands several times, when it became the property of Smith and Allnutt. In 1895 Henry Allnut and Son operated it until its closure in the early 1960s.

Upper Tovil Mill possibly dates back to 1650; by 1681 it was certainly a paper mill, that was regularly to change hands during the next 200 years. In the 1860s straw was used as the raw material for paper, hence nearby Straw Mill Hill. In 1894 Albert E. Reed of Exeter came to live in Kent, and in 1896 bought the remains of Upper Tovil Mill, as it had recently been burnt down. Reed fitted steam engines and modernised the mill. In 1905 he purchased the nearby Bridge Mill, which in 1551 belonged to Lord Cobham and had seen a variety of uses from fulling and gunpowder production to linseed oil. In 1922 Albert E. Reed opened a modern paper mill at Aylesford, the first of the developments that were to become Reed International.

Hayle Mill is first mentioned in 1627 though a mill has probably existed on the site since before 1500. In 1722 the mill was bought by Thomas Pine and in 1805 John Pine built the present mill. In 1812 this was bought by John Green, a paper maker, whose family had been in the trade since c1680. The mill has not always prospered but has managed to remain in the care of the Green family, and is now one of the few remaining hand-made paper mills.

The siting of so many paper mills in such a small geographical area arose from several factors. There had to be swift-running water to provide power for a water wheel, and water which was pure so that it did not discolour the paper. Rags from which paper was made were available from Maidstone and London, and old ropes and canvas from Chatham were also used. Communications were good, barges taking paper up to London, returning with a load of rags.

The introduction of steam speeded the processes involved, and Hayle Mill certainly had a steam boiler by 1838, though Turkey Mill had used its beam engine since 1807.

The repeal of paper tax in 1861 greatly increased demand. Wood pulp came into use and mills which were not mechanised faced closure. Today Maidstone is perhaps unique in that it boasts both modern mechanical production and the traditional skills and methods.

Several local printing firms such as Alabaster Passmore and Son Ltd are based in the area, originally encouraged by the availability of paper.

The mediaeval Wealden iron industry did not spread as far as Maidstone until later. The Medway Foundry of St Peter Street, Maidstone, made iron water wheels in the 1780s. Engineering companies such as Drake and Fletcher, founded in 1898, or Haynes and Son (1856) sold and repaired motor vehicles, as did Tilling and Stevens Ltd, founded in 1897. Beginning in 1906 by adapting a dynamo to provide power for touring cars, then developing 'buses, the company quickly expanded. In 1938 it acquired Vulcan Motors of Huddersfield, all production being moved to Maidstone. In 1952 Tilling and Stevens were taken over by Rootes, who were in turn to become part of Chrysler UK Ltd. The works finally closed in 1977.

The rich supply of fruit grown in the area led to the development of a local canning industry, while grocery businesses expanded into food manufacturing. In 1889 Foster Clark experimented in the production of cake flours, soon opening his own firm in Mote Way. In 1898 his firm bought part of the Charlmers Jam Factory, which was based in Hart Street. After becoming a public company in 1929 Foster Clark's became well known for custard powder, soups, gravy powder and their Eiffel Tower trade mark. After the Second World War the firm declined to eventual closure. The company founded by Edward Sharp is known world wide. In about 1892 Mr Sharp began to make sweets which he sold in his grocer's shop in Week Street. The confectionery proved popular and in 1897 a small sweet factory was opened in Sandling Road. These premises proved too small, and when the engineering works of Messrs Jesse Ellis and Co of St Peter's Street became vacant, the company moved to this site. Situated conveniently beside the Medway, sugar was brought to the factory by barge. Now called Trebor Sharps the firm continues to manufacture sweets, ingredients and products now travelling by road. For reasons of access a molasses factory was once sited at Tovil, probably giving rise to the local legend of treacle mines.

Today's Maidstone continues to be a thriving market town, with a variety of shops that draw in trade from the surrounding areas. It is also a centre for insurance, banking and local government. The Kent Insurance Company dates back to 1802, in 1901 becoming part of the Royal Insurance Group. In the late 1700s the town had two banks, from which the New Kentish Bank was founded in 1818, since 1970 part of the National Westminster Bank. County Hall, built in 1913, formalised county administration here, and became a major local employer.

With its variety of trade and commerce, Maidstone continues to grow, several of its products world famous.

This combination of modern manufacturing and service industries, the continuing focus the town provides for trade in the surrounding area, its pre-eminence in county government and its rich heritage promise a prosperous and civilised future for the County Town of Kent.

Maidstone from the London Road. In the foreground people
are resting from harvesting.

ABOVE: The river has always been important to Maidstone, especially when the Medway was busy with water traffic and the boat builder was in demand. CENTRE: A 'set' of hop pickers at work at the turn of the century. BELOW: Unloading greenbags at Boughton.

138

ABOVE LEFT: View from the Undercliff showing the Medway Brewery after 1899, when it was owned by Style and Winch. BELOW: The Sun Inn on Middle Row, originally called The Swan. RIGHT: A tally man cuts a notch on his and the pickers tally stick. CENTRE LEFT: The depot of the Fremlins Brewery built in 1887. RIGHT: Jesse Ellis, the owner of an engineering works in St Peter's Street, with one of his engines. (MM) BELOW: In the 1860s fulling mills in the Loose Valley converted to papermaking.

ABOVE: In 1894 Albert E. Reed came to live in Kent and developed a paper making concern which became one of the town's largest employers. BELOW LEFT: The Golden Boot has drawn generations of Maidstone folk to F. W. Randall & Co. In earlier days this shop was especially busy when hopping ended and new shoes could be afforded for the winter. RIGHT: Since the late 1700s banking has been an important part of the town's commerce. The Kentish Bank, now the National Westminster, moved to this grand building, designed by W. Campbell-Jones, in 1909.

Index

142

Subscribers

Presentation copies

1 Maidstone Borough Council
2 Kent County Council
3 Maidstone Library
4 Kent County Library
5 Maidstone Museums & Art Gallery
6 Gordon Bonner FRIBA

7   Hilary C. Watson
8   Clive & Carolyn Birch
9   L.R.A. Grove
10 Mrs J.M. Burgess
11
12 M.C. Cradduck
13 Mr & Mrs John N. Horne
14 Miss L. McKenzie Smith
15 Miss E.M. Attwood
16 J.H. Farrant
17 J.R. Dann
18 H.B. Tyson
19 Mrs N.C. Quickenden
20 Eric Smith
21 P.W. Thompson
22 Mrs V. Arnold
23 L. Slater
24 A. Passmore
25 Mrs R.F. Hood
26 P. Grenyer
27 R.G. Clegg
28 Mrs H.L. Uden
29 Mrs L.R. Stratton
30 Michael R. Craft
31 Alan L. Capon
32 J.J. Brakefield
33 Mrs M.J. Chapman
34 Miss Fiona Bryan
35 J. Anders
36 Peter Chard
37 David Read
38 Malcolm Read
39 Victoria & Albert Museum
40 Leicester Library
41 B.S. Kiek
42 Mrs M. Chapman
43 Miss A.J. Jellis
44 Mrs Joan Olive Wood
45 Mrs S. Thomson
46 Mrs S.D. Luckhurst
47 Andrew J. Clark

48 M.T. Bowling
49 B. King
50 I.A. Coulson
51 S.P. Newbery
52 F. Hands
53 P.R. Green
54 M.J. Whitson

55 Mrs Irene Hales
56 M.R. Glover
57 N.C. Milsted
58 E.W. Harrison
59 E. Clifford
60 D.G. Elliott
61 Peter D. Royall
62 Gerald W. Watson
63 Mrs Rita Norris
64 P.J. Bennett
65 C.C.L. Hitchcock
66 Piers A. Bennett
67 R. Birchall
68 Mrs A. Dixon
69 Mrs J. Moir
70 D.P. Cooke
71 R.F.M. Hawkins
72 Mrs Pamela Bishop
73 S.R: Cameron
74 Mrs J. Simon
75
76 Miss D. Woodrow
77 Peter Salway
78 Ian M.T. Wigston
79 Mrs O.J. Stallion
80 Gordon Stone
81 T. Thorpe
82 Mrs I.R. Brown
83 G.A. Wisden
84 Mrs D.H. Eldridge
85 A.R. Thomsett
86 R.K. Clapham
87 Dr N.P. Hudd
88 Mrs M.E. Hudd
89 Alan C. Henderson
90 E.R. Green
91 Jim McQuillan
92 James Saunders
93 John H. Day
94 R.P. Collins
95 Mrs E. Jones
96 Mrs I. Whitbourne
97 E.M. Blennerhassett
98 Mrs E. Seath
99 Captain G.A. Simmons
100
101 E.W. Cooper
102 Mrs S.A. File

103 Mrs D. Margerum
104 Miss J.S. Phippard
105 Mrs Wendy Cooper
106 Michael John Daniel
107 Yuri Roovet
108 Mrs D.M. Battye
109 Dr Rosalind Bearcroft
110 Bernard A. Sancto
111 Margaret Lawrence
112 P.J. Orpin
113 M.W. Orpin
114 W. Haynes
115 N. Swift
116 A.J. King
117 Mr & Mrs J. Chesney
118 Mrs Jean Cross
119 K. Ferris
120 P.D. Edwards
121 Mrs L.M. Prior
122 E.A. Robinson
123 R.F. Wicken
124 Mrs E.D. Worrall
125 S. Woodgate
126 D.F. Tully
127 B.G. Thomas
128 H.V. Summerton
129 Mrs D.V. Andrews
130 N.C. Earl
131 Mrs R. Waters
132 R.C. Adams
133 Mrs J. Hollands
134 Mrs M. Waller
135 G. Linton-Smith
136 I. Horton
137 A.D. Short
138 J. Clinch
139 B.C. King
140 R.V. & P. Cook
141 D. Kingsman
142 K. Blackman
143 P. & J.M. McGlennon
144 Miss D.L.B. Abnett
145 Miss A.E. Newman
146 Mrs B.J. Griffiths
147 Mrs P. Shepherd
148 Mrs V.E. Peachey
149 Mrs O. Case
150 Mrs V.P. Kavanagh

151 Mrs J. Sutton
152 J.W. Harris
153 Mrs K.G. Skene
154 The Maplesden Noakes School
155 Miss J. Kelsey
156 M.E. Brian
157 Mrs C. Dudley
158 Mrs M. Balcomb
159 J. Swade
160 B.J. Aldridge
161 Oldborough Manor School
162 K.A.E. Wells
163 Mrs K.P. Smith
164 Alan Hobbs
165 Miss G. Batt
166 Mrs J.M. Thorpe
167 P.E. Bannister
168 Miss E. Harris
169 Mrs P. Pentecost
170 A.A. Monk
171 Maidstone Adult Education Centre
172 H. Chalton
173 Madginford Park Junior School
174 A.C. Parfitt
175 Mrs D. Salmon
176 Malcolm Victor Gladwin
177 R.F. Ambrose
178 R.S. Romain
179 Mrs S. Carver
180 Mrs M. Horrocks
181 Miss H. Rooke
182 Mrs J. Belworthy
183 C.W. Tutt
184 Pamela Dann
185 Jean Goble
186 Mrs V.H. Hills
187 H. Lyon
188 J.M. Heaton
189 Mrs R.W. Hull
190 Mrs P.I. Foster
191 Mr & Mrs C.J. Hollingsnead
192 R.S. Izett
193 J.W. Moubray
194 H.E. Warner
195 B.J. Cornish
196 Mrs N. Ranger
197 David Asprey
198 Christopher Delgev
199 J.R. Lyons
200 Reg & Sylvia Burrows
201
251 Kent County Library HQ
252 Stoneborough Centre
253 Arthur Potter
254
255 D.W. Freeman
256 John Bradford
257 Miss L. Hill
258 H.E. Orpin
259
260 H.C. Watson
261 C.J. Wade
262 K.W.E. Gravett
263 K.C. Yates-Smith
264 G.G. Howe
265 Miss D.E. Boseley
266 Mrs G. King
267 Edward H. Schofield
268 M.E. Noonan
269 G.W.J. Collins
270 Dennis Root
271 R. Bonny
272 W.R. Sharp
273 Mrs E. Birch
274 D.A. Gruber
275 Mrs B. Lomay
276
277 Mrs B. Gates
278 M.J. Collins
279 A.H. Pudney
280 Nicholas Sands
281 Mrs J. Thomson
282 R.H. Hilton JP
283 J.H. Goodsell
284 S.F. Lewis
285 Mrs R. Cooney
286 Christopher Axon
287 Mrs J. Harling
288 N. Crafts
289 Miss K.M. Wells
290 Mrs I. Abrahams
291 Paul Ledger
292 D. Mason
293 P.B. Roberts
294 Dawn Capeling
295 E.S. Tinsley
296 Mrs Evelyn Seath
297 Miss E.A. Dubbins
298 G.L. Paterson
299 Leslie E. Bray
300 W. Barden
301 G.M. Britter
302
304 Mrs M. Morrison
305 A.J. Saunders
306 Miss J.A. Mallett
307 R.G. Smith
308 Mrs Marie Hawkins
309 Mrs D. Mansfield
310 R.M. Hensby
311
314 Councillor C.W. Playford
315 Mrs A.J. Daniels
316 J.R.E. Sharp
317 Fred S. Wood
318 Senacre Wood C.P. School
319 Mrs J. Branch
320 Miss Janet S. Phippard
321 North Borough C.P. School
322
323 Stanley H. Walker
324 Laurence B. Fermor
325 St Simon Stock School
326
327 Mr Cheesman
328 South Borough C.P. School
329 Oldborough Manor School
330
331 K.A. Williams
332 J. Bynoe
333 R.E. Sears
334 Maidstone School for Girls
335 Cox Heath C.P. Infant School
336 Jean Goble
337 Paul Oldham
338 Reg & Sylvia Burrows
339
341 Loose C.P. Junior School
342 Maj-Gen The Viscount Monckton of Brenchley, CB, OBE, MC, OL
343 N.C. Hawkins
344 Roy C. Beale
345 H.J. Green
346 Cecil N. Cullingford
347 A. Boakes
348 F. Brook
349
350 A.J. Bignell
351 Ann J. Winser
352 R.L. Hickman
353 J.B. Flaskman
354 L.G. Rookledge
355 Mrs K.M. Wolf
356 Mrs M. Pooley
357 Mr & Mrs B.G. Watson

Remaining names unlisted.

The following pictures are reproduced by permission of The Mansell Collection: The Peasants' Revolt (p36); Jack Cade (p37) and Elizabeth Woodville (p44).

ENDPAPERS: FRONT – Map of Kent, 1719. Engraved by Samuel Parker for John Harris' *History of Kent* published in 1719, based on Philip Symonson's map of Kent, 1596. BACK – Map of the Hundred of Maidstone.

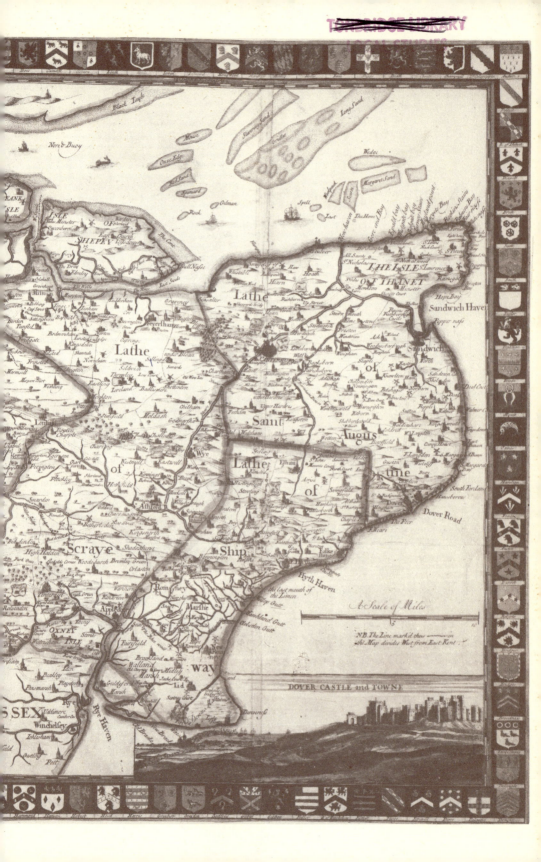